陳 Helen's
Asian
Kitchen®

easy
chinese
stir-fries

easy
chinese
stir-fries

helen chen

photography by jason wyche

WILEY

JOHN WILEY & SONS, INC.

Published by John Wiley & Sons, Inc., Hoboken, New Jersey
Published simultaneously in Canada

Book design by Elizabeth Van Itallie
Food styling by Jamie Kimm
Prop styling by Leslie Siegel

The publisher wishes to thank Pearl River Mart, 477 Broadway, New York, NY 10013, 212–431–4770, www.pearlriver.com, for their generous contribution of props for the photographs on the following pages: 32 (bowl), 41 (sake cups), 45 (chopsticks), 62 (chopsticks), 83 (bowl), 86 (bowl), 98 (wooden spoon), 103 (bowl), and 108 (bowl, sake set).
Thank you to Harold Import Company, Inc. for providing the cookware props.
Some of these recipes have been previously published in *Helen Chen's Chinese Home Cooking* (1994).

Library of Congress Cataloging-in-Publication Data:
Chen, Helen.
[Asian kitchen]
Helen's Asian kitchen: easy Chinese stir-fries / Helen Chen; photography by Jason Wyche.
p. cm.
Includes index.
ISBN 978–0–470–38756–6 (cloth)
1. Cookery, Chinese. 2. Cookery, Asian. 3. Stir frying. I. Title. II. Title: Asian kitchen.
TX724.5.C5C5372 2009
641.5951—dc22
2008027969
Printed in China
10 9 8 7 6 5 4 3 2 1

This book is dedicated in loving memory to my brother, Henry T.M. Chen.

contents

foreword

I was born in Shanghai, China, and grew up in Cambridge, Massachusetts. Worlds apart, yet linked through the traditional upbringing I received from my parents; especially from my mother, Joyce Chen, who handed down to me the traditions and culture she learned from her mother and father in Beijing.

I learned to cook the old-fashioned way, from my mother. When I was growing up, my mother did all of the cooking at home and the variety was endless. There were festival foods, seasonal specialties, and those infrequent dishes that were either very labor-intensive or required hard-to-get ingredients. But it was her everyday Chinese home cooking that I remember best—the often revisited stir-fry dishes that are simple, easy, delicious, and part of the culinary repertoire of most Chinese families.

I hope you will enjoy this collection of some of my favorites. Perhaps some will become part of your everyday cooking too. So, come with me to my kitchen and let me share with you what the Chinese do in theirs.

—Helen Chen

techniques

Stir-frying is a cooking technique that is unique to and synonymous with Chinese cuisine. It is believed that it began during the Han dynasty over two thousand years ago in response to the lack of adequate fuel. Stir-frying requires quick, intense heat and short, rapid cooking. Uniform, bite-size pieces of food are rapidly sautéed in a small amount of hot oil with various sauces and spices for flavor. This not only conserved valuable fuel, but also retained nutrients and vitamins found naturally in foods. When time is limited, stir-frying is one of the best and fastest ways to prepare a meal and one of the most healthful too.

Stir-frying is not difficult, but there are a few things to keep in mind that will greatly increase the success as well as the enjoyment of this age-old cooking technique.

cooking oils

I always use canola oil in all of my Chinese cooking, whether I stir-fry or deep-fry. Of the commonly used cooking oils, canola oil is lowest in saturated (bad) fat, high in mono-unsaturated (good) fat, and is a good source for omega-3 fatty acids. It has no taste of its own, can withstand the high temperatures needed for stir-frying, and is inexpensive and easily available. However, if you wish you may also use vegetable, corn, soy bean, or peanut oil.

You do not need a great deal of oil to stir-fry, especially if you are using a good-quality nonstick pan or a well-seasoned carbon steel wok. Generally I recommend about three tablespoons of oil for a dish that serves four people. A little oil, however, does not mean you can use cooking oil sprays. That's not enough oil, not even for a nonstick pan.

I don't recommend that the oil be superheated to the smoking point; that is, the point in which the oil begins to burn. Smoking oil is burning oil and when the oil is overheated it can be damaged. To test the oil temperature for stir-frying, I use this simple technique: Place the tip of a wooden or bamboo spatula in the oil; bubbles will form if the oil is hot enough. I sometimes dip the end of the spatula in the moist ingredients; then the spatula not only bubbles but sizzles too. Also, adding aromatics such as garlic and ginger in the oil can be used as a gauge. When the aromatics sizzle, then the oil is ready.

why is cornstarch important?

Marinating meats and seafood with a little wine and cornstarch before cooking helps to seal in the juices, keeping the ingredients moist and tender when stir-fried. And because cornstarch quickly creates a translucent, thickened sauce, it is perfect for the rapid cooking style of stir-frying. (Flour, on the other hand, requires a longer cooking time to remove that raw, flour taste.) When using cornstarch to thicken sauces and gravies, always mix it thoroughly with a little water before adding to hot liquids.

how much heat?

Most of the stir-fry recipes in this book call for medium-high or high temperatures. It's best to start at medium-high and adjust up or down accordingly. If the food appears to be cooking too rapidly or is beginning to burn, stick, or scorch, turn down the heat or remove the pan from the heat. I often add some water or broth, which brings down the temperature immediately and creates a little extra gravy as a bonus.

I do not recommend that a nonstick pan be preheated before adding the oil. Preheating an uncoated steel pan is fine, but with nonstick cookware, heating up an empty pan may actually damage the coating.

mise en place

Mise en place is a French term used by professional chefs to mean having all of the ingredients prepared and ready before you start cooking. Reading the recipe through and having all of the ingredients cut, measured, and available is a good habit to establish, especially for stir-frying, which is such a rapid cooking technique. Organize the ingredients in small dishes or bowls so that everything is within your reach. Also, have your serving dish chosen and set out as well.

hints for successful, stress-free stir-frying

When stir-frying, put the food in the pan according to which ingredients take longest to cook. Hard ingredients such as root vegetables and cabbage, for example, are put in first, with the more delicate fast-cooking ingredients such as snow peas and bean sprouts added last. In some cases, the vegetables are partially cooked first, removed from the pan, and then added back in after the meat or seafood is almost cooked through.

Do not overload your pan. A pan with too much food will cool down rapidly and never quite recover for proper stir-frying. If you are doubling or tripling the recipe, it is best to cook the dish two times rather than all at once.

Most stir-fried foods should be removed from the pan and served immediately. People should wait for the food, not the food for the people. When my mother prepared dinner, we had to be at the table when she brought the dishes out of the kitchen. That way, each dish could be enjoyed at its peak. Nor should guests wait for the cook. The person cooking is always the last to come to the table.

serving a chinese meal

For casual Chinese-style dinners at home, all of the dishes, including the soup and rice, are served at once at the center of the table. The number of dishes depends on the number of guests, but in general for simple home meals, two or three well-chosen dishes with rice and sometimes a soup is perfectly adequate. Since many stir-fried dishes combine meat with vegetables, a single recipe also makes a delicious one-dish meal.

When choosing which dishes to cook, keep in mind that what you want is a well-balanced meal that combines a variety of ingredients, such as meat or seafood with vegetables. A combination of tastes and textures is also important; so a sweet-and-sour dish should be served with a savory one and a crispy, fried dish should be served with a soft textured dish, such as bean curd.

equipment

The traditional Chinese kitchen is a rather Spartan place, and it's hard to believe that a few simple hand tools and a single pan could produce such incredible delicacies. These few kitchen tools often confuse most Western cooks partly because so much misinformation abounds. There is no substitute for good-quality cooking equipment, and since in the Chinese kitchen there is literally one pan and one knife, it makes sense to buy the best you can afford.

It is not essential that you have everything listed, but it certainly makes the job much easier, safer, and more enjoyable to have the proper tools.

the wok or stir-fry pan

My preference is for either a 14-inch flat-bottom wok, or 12-inch flat-bottom stir-fry pan with single skillet-style handles. The flat bottom eliminates the need for a ring stand and allows the pan to sit securely on any gas or electric burner and concentrates the heat at the center of the pan. If cooking on an electric burner—coils, halogen, or induction—a flat-bottom wok is essential. A long, single handle makes it far easier and safer to move the pan and pick it up when you are transferring the food to a serving platter.

Traditional Chinese woks are generally made of carbon steel. Choose a good-quality heavyweight pan to ensure even heat conduction.

uncoated carbon steel or nonstick?

Some people prefer the traditional carbon steel that must be seasoned on a regular basis to prevent rusting and to create a black patina on the inside of the pan. I find, however, that most people do not use their woks often enough to keep the seasoned patina in tiptop shape. Chinese people use the wok many times

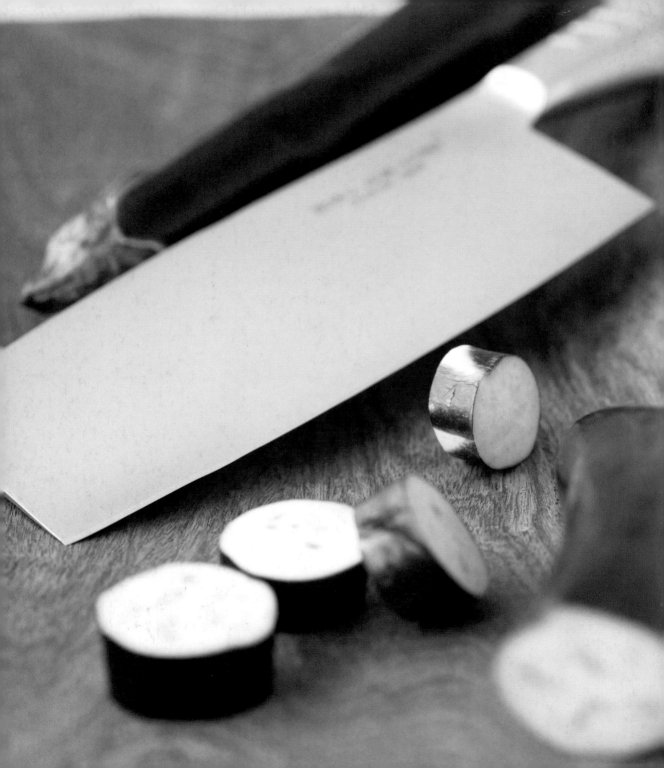

every day; it is constantly being cooked in, cleaned, and reseasoned. The complaint about tacky, dusty, and rancid oil on rusted woks is a result of underuse. With an uncoated carbon steel wok, the more you use it, the better it gets. So, if you plan to use your wok regularly and don't mind the ritual of seasoning, an uncoated carbon steel pan is fine for you.

seasoning a carbon steel wok

When the wok is new, the protective oil or lacquer coating must be scrubbed and thoroughly cleaned off before seasoning can begin. When the inside of the wok is clean, rinse and dry the pan thoroughly and season immediately or the wok will begin to rust.

Pour 1 to 2 teaspoons of cooking oil (such as canola, vegetable, soybean, or peanut oil but not butter or olive oil) into the wok and smear the oil over the entire inside of the pan using a clean paper towel. Place the pan over medium heat and heat it up slowly. Allow the pan to smoke while rubbing in the oil for 15 to 30 seconds, tilting the wok over the burner so that the sides of the wok heat up as well as the bottom. The pan will be hot, so handle with care. Repeat the oiling and heating process 3 or 4 times, letting the pan cool in between each oiling. Your wok now has its initial seasoning and is ready to use.

To continue to develop and maintain your wok, rinse the pan with hot water after each use and if necessary gently scrub away clinging food particles with a brush or non-metallic scrubber. Use dishwashing liquid only if necessary, as it may strip away some of the seasoning. Rinse the pan and dry thoroughly. Place the wok over medium-high heat to finish drying and wipe a very thin film of cooking oil over the inside of the wok to prevent incidental rusting while in storage and to help maintain the seasoned surface. If rust appears, simply scrub it away, rinse and dry the pan, and season it again.

Nonstick pans, on the other hand, do not require seasoning nor do they require frequent use. But all nonsticks are not equal. Many nonstick coatings do not tolerate the high-heat demands of stir-frying. They may be great for flipping pancakes or frying eggs but eventually fail as woks. There are a number of newer, high-quality, reinforced nonstick coatings that not only hold up well to high temperatures, but to constant stirring as well. These durable nonstick coatings are found on higher-quality woks and stir-fry pans. I personally use nonstick woks and stir-fry pans, and I have had excellent results with Excalibur®, a reinforced nonstick finish applied on higher-quality pans. I heartily recommend it.

I do not recommend electric woks. They generally do not provide enough heat for proper stir-frying, and they are difficult to control since the heating element is part of the pan itself.

the chinese knife

Just as important as a good wok is a good knife. Notice that I didn't say "cleaver." I really mean a Chinese chef knife; this is what is needed for the slicing, dicing, and cutting of boneless meat and vegetables. For stir-frying it is imperative that the ingredients be cut in uniform size so they cook quickly and evenly. Cleavers are made for chopping, while the Chinese chef knife is for cutting. The Chinese chef knife is a medium-weight knife that is traditionally designed with a wide, rectangular blade and wooden or metal handle.

I prefer a high-quality stainless-steel knife. Stainless is much easier to maintain and won't rust, stain, or give a metallic taste to foods. A good knife should feel comfortable in your hand— well-balanced and solid—with a handle that will not absorb oils or juices from raw meat.

A Chinese knife should be cared for like any other good knife. It should never be placed in the dishwasher. Store it carefully so the blade does not rub up against hard objects that will chip or dull its edge. Use a sharpening steel occasionally to hone the edge.

the wire strainer

This long bamboo-handled woven wire strainer has been adopted by both Western and Asian cooks and is affectionately nicknamed "the spider" because of its fine, weblike wire mesh. The wide basket strains everything from pasta to vegetables to dumplings quickly and thoroughly.

the spatula

I like bamboo spatulas because they are strong, durable, and gentle to any cooking surface and they are dishwasher-safe. Unlike plastic spatulas that can soften and become flexible when heated, bamboo spatulas stay stiff for more efficient and less fatiguing stir-frying. Choose spatulas with rounded corners so they reach into the rounded sides of woks and stir-fry pans.

the ginger grater

In most stir-fry recipes the ginger is simply sliced and tossed in; however, in some cases grated ginger is called for. Made of stainless steel or porcelain, Asian ginger graters have sharp raised teeth that pull out the ginger pulp while leaving the tough strings behind. A little bamboo brush is also available to help dislodge the ginger and clean the grater.

chopsticks

I always have table or cooking chopsticks in the kitchen for mixing, beating, stirring, or picking up little morsels for tasting or removing ginger and garlic pieces from dishes after cooking. Natural bamboo chopsticks are inexpensive, durable, and easiest to use.

ingredients

BEAN CURD (*Doufu* in Chinese, and *tofu* in Japanese) is made from soy beans and is rather bland in flavor but takes on the taste of the sauce in which it is cooked. It's a healthy alternative to meat since it contains a high amount of protein and calcium without fat. For stir-frying I use firm Chinese-style bean curd rather than the soft or "silken" tofu.

BOK CHOY There are many varieties, but two are most commonly used. The first, readily available in most supermarkets, has thick, crunchy white stalks with dark green leaves. The other variety of bok choy, one of my favorites, is Shanghai bok choy, sometimes called baby bok choy. Instead of the stiff white stems and dark green leaves of the more common supermarket bok choy, Shanghai bok choy is smaller and more compact, about 6 inches long, and has delicate lighter green stems and leaves.

CHINESE RICE WINE In Chinese cooking, rice wine is often used as a seasoning to cover up certain unwanted flavors, like fishiness from seafood. Shaoxing wine, from Zhejiang Province, is a famous high-quality rice wine used for both cooking and drinking. Chinese rice wines sold for cooking are available in Chinese grocery stores. Chinese cooking wines are salted so don't use them as a table wine. An excellent, and often used, substitute is pale dry sherry.

DRIED BLACK MUSHROOMS These are shiitake mushrooms that have been dried. The Chinese like to use them dried because the smoky flavor is more concentrated. Before use they must be soaked in water until pliable and the woody stems removed. They can be found in most Asian markets.

DRIED WOOD EAR Also known as black fungus, wood ears are a kind of black, gelatinous fungus that grows on trees. They are appreciated for their crisp texture and not for their flavor, of which there is little. Look for small, black flakes, about half an inch or smaller in size,

not the large pieces with grayish color on one side, which tend to be tough. They can be found in most Asian markets.

FERMENTED BLACK BEANS (SALTED BLACK BEANS) Not to be confused with dried black beans, these are whole soy beans that have been salted and aged with spices. They have a rich, robust, salty taste and tender texture and can be found in most Asian markets.

GARLIC CHIVES Also known as Chinese chives or *jiu cai* in Mandarin, these long, grasslike leaves are flat rather than round and have a stronger flavor and texture than regular chives. Garlic chives is a perennial plant and is easy to grow. If unable to find, you can substitute scallions.

DRIED GOLDEN NEEDLES (DRIED LILY BUDS) These dried unopened blossoms of a certain species of day lily are used in vegetarian and northern-style dishes. The dried flowers must be softened in hot water, the hard stem knob cut off, and excess water squeezed out. Look for light brown supple buds; if they are hard, dark, or black, they are too old.

FRESH GINGER An irregularly shaped, fibrous rhizome. Look for a smooth, shiny, tan-colored skin and firm, rock-hard root. Do not substitute ground ginger.

HOISIN SAUCE This versatile soy bean sauce, which is flavored with spices and garlic and sweetened, is used in cooking and as a dipping sauce for dishes served with Mandarin pancakes, such as Moo Shi Pork and Peking Duck.

CHINESE HOT BEAN PASTE (BEAN SAUCE) A thick, salty, fermented bean paste made with soy beans, flour, chiles, salt, and sugar, it comes packed in cans or small jars. It is commonly used as a base in spicy Sichuan dishes and can be found in most Asian markets. A good brand is from Szechuan Food Products Co., Ltd., called Hot Bean Sauce.

**NAPA CABBAGE
(TIANJIN CABBAGE)**

Napa cabbage is a variety of Chinese cabbage that is pale green with crinkly leaves and a tight compact shape. I always have a head of napa in my refrigerator because it's a great emergency ingredient. It keeps well in the refrigerator, can be used in a variety of dishes, and has a fresh, mild taste that's not cabbagey at all. Chinese celery cabbage, the long cylindrical cousin to napa, may be substituted if napa is not available.

OYSTER SAUCE

This versatile and tasty Cantonese cooking sauce, also called oyster-flavored sauce, is made from oyster extract, salt, and spices. Contrary to its name, this thick brown sauce does not taste like oysters.

SESAME OIL

Asian sesame oil is pressed from roasted sesame seeds, hence its dark amber color and fragrance. Since this oil has a low smoking temperature and is strongly flavored, it is not suitable for stir frying, but is used as a garnishing oil or for making dressings and dips or added to fillings for flavor.

SICHUAN PEPPERCORNS

Unrelated to black peppercorns, these dried reddish-brown berries are widely used in Sichuan cuisine for seasoning, as well as for pickling and curing meats. They are generally toasted and ground before use.

SOY SAUCE

Soy sauces from China are recommended. There are two main kinds of soy sauce used in Chinese cooking—light and dark. Light soy sauce, not to be confused with the low-salt soy sauce sold in many supermarkets these days, refers to the thin texture of the sauce and may be substituted with a Japanese soy sauce. Dark soy sauce contains molasses, which gives it a darker color, slightly sweeter taste, and thicker texture. I always keep both types handy.

chicken

chicken with mixed garden vegetables

You can use many kinds of vegetables for this dish, but I like this particular mix because the colors are bright and the flavors combine well with the chicken. Since there is no soy sauce in this recipe, the colors of the vegetables and the chicken shine right through. ✳ **SERVES 3 TO 4**

---

1 tablespoon cornstarch

2 teaspoons Chinese rice wine or dry sherry

1 pound skinless boneless chicken breast, cut into ¾-inch cubes

3 tablespoons canola oil

1 carrot, thinly sliced on the diagonal

2 celery stalks, cut on the diagonal into ¼-inch slices

1 medium red bell pepper, cored and cut into 1½-inch chunks

½ pound bok choy or Shanghai bok choy, cut into 2-inch chunks (about 3 cups)

½ cup canned chicken broth or water

2 slices unpeeled fresh ginger

1 teaspoon salt, or to taste

1 In a medium bowl, whisk together the cornstarch and wine. Add the chicken and mix well.

2 In a wok or stir-fry pan, heat 1 tablespoon of the oil over high heat until the oil is hot but not smoking. Test by dipping a piece of carrot into the oil; it should sizzle. Add all the vegetables and cook, stirring, for about 2 minutes. Add the broth, stir, and cover. Reduce the heat to medium and steam until the vegetables are tender-crisp, about 2 minutes. Transfer the vegetables and their juices to a platter.

3 Add the remaining 2 tablespoons of oil to the same pan and heat over high heat. Add the ginger and salt and stir until the oil is hot and ginger sizzles. Stir up the chicken mixture and add it to the pan. Cook, stirring, until the chicken turns white and is almost done, 2 to 3 minutes.

4 Return the vegetables and any juices to the pan, mix thoroughly, and cook until vegetables are heated and chicken is cooked through, about 1 minute. Taste and add more salt, as needed. Remove and discard the ginger, if desired. Transfer the chicken and vegetables to a platter. Serve immediately.

chicken with mushrooms and snow peas

If you want to make this recipe a little more exotic, use half fresh and half dried black mushrooms. Soften the dried mushrooms in hot water for about 15 minutes, trim the stems, and cut the caps into pieces similar in size to the fresh mushrooms. You may also try other kinds of fresh mushrooms, such as porcini or shiitake.

✳ SERVES 3 TO 4

1 teaspoon Chinese rice wine or dry sherry

2 teaspoons cornstarch

1½ teaspoons salt

1 pound skinless boneless chicken breast, cut into ¾-inch cubes

3 tablespoons canola oil

2 slices unpeeled fresh ginger

1 garlic clove, crushed with the side of a knife and peeled

¾ pound fresh button mushrooms, cleaned and quartered (about 2 cups)

¾ pound snow peas, ends snapped off and strings removed (about 2 cups)

1 (8-ounce) can sliced bamboo shoots, drained

1 In a medium bowl, whisk together the wine, 1 teaspoon of the cornstarch, and salt. Add the chicken and mix well. Dissolve the remaining teaspoon of cornstarch in 1 tablespoon water.

2 In a wok or stir-fry pan, heat the oil over high heat. Add the ginger and garlic and stir until the oil is hot and the ginger and garlic sizzle.

3 Stir up the chicken mixture and add it to the pan. Cook, stirring constantly, until the chicken turns white, about 2 minutes. Add the mushrooms, snow peas, and bamboo shoots. Continue stirring until the snow peas turn a darker green, about 1 minute.

4 Stir up the cornstarch mixture, making sure it is completely dissolved, and add it to the pan. Continue stirring until the liquid thickens and the chicken is cooked through. Remove and discard the ginger and garlic, if desired. Serve immediately.

chicken with broccoli and bamboo shoots

Fresh broccoli always gives the best results. If you are rushed, you can get precut raw broccoli at the supermarket salad bar. It may cost a little more, but it's better than using frozen broccoli. ✳ **SERVES 3 TO 4**

---

1 pound broccoli

2 teaspoons cornstarch

2 teaspoons Chinese rice wine or dry sherry

1 pound skinless boneless chicken breast, cut into ¾-inch cubes

3 tablespoons dark soy sauce

3 tablespoons hoisin sauce

1½ teaspoons sugar

4 tablespoons canola oil

2 slices unpeeled fresh ginger

1 garlic clove, crushed with the side of a knife and peeled

1 (8-ounce) can sliced bamboo shoots, drained

1 teaspoon sesame oil

1 Trim and peel the broccoli stalks. Chop the flower heads from the stalks and cut into florets. Slice the peeled stalks into bite-size pieces.

2 In a medium bowl, whisk together the cornstarch and wine. Add the chicken and mix well.

3 In a small bowl, whisk together the soy sauce, hoisin sauce, sugar, and 2 tablespoons water.

4 In a wok or stir-fry pan, heat 1 tablespoon of the canola oil over high heat until hot but not smoking. Test by dipping a piece of broccoli in the oil; it should sizzle. Add the broccoli and cook, stirring, for about 30 seconds. Stir in 3 tablespoons water, reduce the heat to medium, and cover the pan. Continue cooking, stirring occasionally, until the broccoli turns a darker green and is tender-crisp, 2 to 3 minutes. Transfer to a shallow dish.

5 Add the remaining 3 tablespoons of canola oil to the same pan and place over high heat. Add the ginger and garlic and stir until the oil is hot and the ginger and garlic sizzle. Stir up the chicken mixture and add it to the pan. Cook, stirring, until the chicken turns white, 1 to 2 minutes. Remove and discard the ginger and garlic, if desired. Reduce the heat to medium and stir in the soy sauce mixture. Add the bamboo shoots, return the broccoli to the pan, and cook, stirring constantly, until all the ingredients are heated and well blended and the chicken is cooked through. Drizzle with sesame oil and mix well. Serve immediately.

mandarin orange chicken

My version of the classic orange chicken requires no deep-frying, so you save time, effort, and calories. I use frozen orange juice concentrate, which blends exceptionally well with the spicy hotness of chiles. If you don't like chiles, you can omit them. Separately stir-frying the snow peas and using them to ring the chicken makes a very nice presentation for dinner parties. For a family meal, you can return the snow peas to the pan just after the oranges and mix them in. ✳ **SERVES 3 TO 4**

---

2 teaspoons Chinese rice wine or dry sherry

3 teaspoons cornstarch

1 pound skinless boneless chicken breast, cut into ¾-inch cubes

2 teaspoons sugar

1 tablespoon cider vinegar

3 tablespoons light soy sauce

3 tablespoons frozen orange juice concentrate

4 tablespoons canola oil

¼ pound snow peas, ends snapped off and strings removed, cut on the diagonal into ½-inch pieces

2 to 4 dried chiles, seeds removed

1 In a medium bowl, whisk together the wine and cornstarch. Add the chicken and mix well. In a separate bowl, combine the sugar, vinegar, soy sauce, and orange juice concentrate and mix well.

2 In a wok or stir-fry pan, heat 1 tablespoon of the oil over medium heat until hot but not smoking. Test by dipping the end of a piece of snow pea in the oil; it should sizzle. Add the snow peas and cook, stirring, just until they turn a darker green, about 30 seconds. Transfer to a large serving platter and spread them out so they will not overcook in their own heat.

3 In the same pan, heat the remaining 3 tablespoons of oil with the chiles over medium heat. As the oil heats up, the peppers will turn dark brown and become very fragrant. Discard the chiles when they are almost black but not burned. Add the garlic and ginger and stir around the pan a few times until they begin to sizzle.

1 garlic clove, crushed with the side of a knife and peeled

2 slices unpeeled fresh ginger

1 (11-ounce) can mandarin oranges, drained

4 Increase the heat to high, stir up the chicken mixture, and add it to the pan. Cook, stirring, for about 1 minute, then add the orange sauce, and continue stirring for another minute or two. When the chicken is almost done, remove and discard the garlic and ginger. Add the mandarin oranges and stir gently to heat through and finish cooking the chicken, not more than 1 minute or the oranges will fall apart.

5 Arrange the snow peas in a ring around the edge of the platter and spoon the chicken and oranges into the center. Serve immediately.

chicken with cashews

This chicken recipe has been an outstanding favorite at our family's landmark Cambridge restaurant for as long as I can remember. There, the cashews are deep-fried, but at home I prefer to toast the nuts instead. This reduces the amount of oil without altering the flavor. ✳ SERVES 3 TO 4

2 teaspoons cornstarch

2 teaspoons Chinese rice wine or dry sherry

½ teaspoon grated peeled fresh ginger

1 pound skinless boneless chicken breast, cut into ¾-inch cubes

2 tablespoons dark soy sauce

2 tablespoons hoisin sauce

1 teaspoon sugar

4 tablespoons canola oil

1 garlic clove, crushed with the side of a knife and peeled

1 cup whole raw cashews, toasted at 350°F oven until fragrant and golden

1 teaspoon sesame oil

1 In a medium bowl, whisk together the cornstarch, wine, and ginger. Add the chicken and mix well.

2 In a small bowl, whisk together the soy sauce, hoisin sauce, sugar, and 2 tablespoons water.

3 In a wok or stir-fry pan, heat the canola oil over high heat. Add the garlic and stir until the oil is hot and the garlic sizzles. Stir up the chicken mixture and add it to the pan. Cook, stirring, until the chicken turn white, 1 to 2 minutes. Remove and discard the garlic, if desired.

4 Reduce the heat to medium and add the soy sauce mixture. Stir until the ingredients are well blended. Add the cashew nuts and stir for another 30 seconds. Drizzle with sesame oil and mix well. Serve immediately.

kung pao chicken

This is a famous Sichuan dish known as *Kung Pao Chi Ting*. At the time of the Qin (pronounced *ch'in*) dynasty, the person in charge of protecting the heir apparent to the throne held the title of "Kung Pao," *kung* meaning "castle" and *pao*, "to protect." During one period, the Kung Pao was a man from Sichuan province whose favorite dish was spicy diced chicken with peanuts. It came to be named after him.

✳ **SERVES 3 TO 4**

---

3 tablespoons dark soy sauce

1 teaspoon salt

1 tablespoon cornstarch

1 pound skinless boneless chicken breasts, cut into ¾-inch cubes

1 teaspoon Chinese rice wine or dry sherry

1 tablespoon sugar

1 tablespoon cider vinegar

1 teaspoon sesame oil

3 tablespoons canola oil

2 to 4 dried chiles, seeds removed

½ teaspoon Sichuan peppercorns, toasted and ground (see Note)

1 garlic clove, sliced

1 In a medium bowl, whisk together 1 tablespoon of the soy sauce, the salt, and cornstarch. Add the chicken and mix well. In a small bowl, whisk together the remaining 2 tablespoons of soy sauce, the wine, sugar, vinegar, and sesame oil.

2 In a wok or stir-fry pan, heat the canola oil over medium-heat. Add the chiles and cook, stirring, until the chiles turn dark brown. Add the peppercorns, garlic, scallion lengths, and ginger and stir for a moment or two.

3 Stir up the chicken mixture and add it to the pan. Cook, stirring briskly, for about 1 minute, then add the soy sauce mixture, the peanuts and the thinly sliced scallions. Turn the heat up to high and cook, stirring, until well mixed, and the chicken is cooked through, about 30 seconds. Remove and discard the chiles and ginger, if desired. Serve immediately.

(continued on page 34)

1 scallion, bulb split, cut into 1½-inch lengths, plus 2 tablespoons thinly sliced scallions

2 slices unpeeled fresh ginger

½ cup unsalted blanched peanuts, toasted, or unsalted dry-roasted peanuts

➤➤ **NOTE:** You may substitute 1 to 3 teaspoons crushed red pepper for the dried chiles. Add with the peppercorns, garlic, and scallions.

➤➤ **NOTE:** To toast Sichuan peppercorns, heat the peppercorns in an ungreased skillet over medium heat until the peppercorns are smoking and fragrant. Do not let them burn. Let the peppercorns cool, then grind them in a mortar and pestle or roll with a rolling pin between two pieces of paper. Sift and discard the larger pieces that do not pass through the strainer. Store the powder in a clean, tightly lidded glass jar in a dark, dry place.

ground chicken and pine nuts in lettuce wraps

Whole lettuce leaves are used as crispy wrappers for the filling. Iceberg or the softer Boston or red or green leaf lettuces work equally well. For a heartier south-of-the-border fusion meal, fill warmed tortillas with shredded lettuce and the turkey filling.

✳ **SERVES 4 AS A MEAL, OR 6 AS APPETIZERS**

---

3 teaspoons cornstarch

1 tablespoon Chinese cooking wine or dry sherry

1 tablespoon light soy sauce

½ pound ground chicken or turkey (1 cup)

1 teaspoon sugar

1 tablespoon hoisin sauce

1 tablespoon dark soy sauce

2 tablespoons canned chicken broth or water

1 teaspoon chili-garlic sauce, or more to taste

8 medium dried black mushrooms, softened in hot water for 15 minutes

½ cup bamboo shoots, diced into ¼ inch cubes

½ cup water chestnuts, diced into ¼ inch cubes

1 In a medium bowl, whisk together 2 teaspoons of the cornstarch, the wine, and light soy sauce. Add the chicken and mix well.

2 In a small bowl, whisk together the remaining 1 teaspoon cornstarch, the sugar, hoisin sauce, dark soy sauce, broth, and chili-garlic sauce.

3 Drain the mushrooms, and squeeze dry. Cut off the stems with scissors and discard. Slice the caps into halves or quarters, if they are large. In a small bowl, combine the mushrooms, bamboo shoots, water chestnuts, celery, pine nuts, peas, and scallions.

4 In a wok or stir-fry pan, heat the canola oil over high heat. Add the ginger and stir until the oil is hot and the ginger sizzles. Add the meat mixture and cook, stirring, until cooked and crumbly, about 2 minutes. Remove and discard the ginger, then add the vegetable mixture. Stir up the sauce mixture, making sure cornstarch is completely dissolved, and add to the pan. Continue stirring for about 1 minute or until the vegetables are heated through and well coated with the sauce. Drizzle with the sesame oil and mix well. Transfer to a platter and serve with lettuce leaves.

(continued on page 37)

ground chicken and pine nuts in lettuce wraps, cont.

½ cup celery, diced into ¼ inch cubes

¼ cup pine nuts (pignoli nuts), toasted in a 325°F oven until lightly browned

½ cup frozen peas, defrosted

3 scallions, thinly sliced

2 tablespoons canola oil

3 slices unpeeled fresh ginger

1 teaspoon sesame oil

8 to 12 whole lettuce leaves, washed and dried

5 To serve, spoon the chicken mixture in the center of a lettuce leaf, fold, and enjoy.

sliced chicken with cucumbers and fermented black beans

This is a dish that I enjoy serving to friends because it always surprises people that cucumbers can be a stir-fry ingredient and that with only the fermented black beans the dish can be so flavorful. ✳ **SERVES 3 TO 4**

---

1 long seedless European cucumber or 1 pound regular cucumbers

3 teaspoons cornstarch

2 teaspoons Chinese rice wine or dry sherry

1 teaspoon salt, or to taste

1 pound skinless boneless chicken breast, cut into 2 x ⅛-inch-thick slices

3 tablespoons canola oil

2 garlic cloves, crushed with the side of a knife and peeled

1 tablespoon fermented black beans, coarsely chopped

1 Wash the cucumber. Seedless European cucumber can be left unpeeled. If using regular cucumbers, peel alternating ½-inch strips of skin lengthwise down the cucumber. Trim away ¾ inch from each end and split lengthwise. With a teaspoon, scrape and discard the seeds or pulp from cucumbers. Slice the cucumbers on the diagonal ½ inch thick. You should have about 4 cups.

2 In a medium bowl, whisk together the cornstarch, wine, and ½ teaspoon salt. Add the chicken and mix well.

3 In a wok or stir-fry pan, heat the oil over high heat. Add the garlic and stir, until the oil is hot and the garlic sizzles. Stir up the chicken mixture and add it to the pan. Cook, stirring briskly, until the chicken is white, 2 to 3 minutes.

4 Add the cucumber slices and cook, stirring, for another 2 minutes. Toss in the black beans and the remaining ½ teaspoon salt and stir until the ingredients and flavors are evenly mixed and the chicken is cooked through. Taste and add more salt, as needed. Remove and discard the garlic, if desired. Serve immediately.

diced almond chicken

Nuts appear frequently in Chinese cooking in desserts, fillings, sweet soups, and stir-fry dishes. The almonds offer a crunchy contrast to the chicken and vegetables. In this dish, all of the ingredients should be diced to about the size of whole almonds. ✳ **SERVES 3 TO 4**

2 teaspoons cornstarch

1 teaspoon Chinese rice wine or dry sherry

1 teaspoon salt, or to taste

1 pound skinless boneless chicken breast, cut into ½-inch cubes

3 tablespoons canola oil

1 slice unpeeled fresh ginger

½ cup canned sliced bamboo shoots, drained and diced

½ cup canned whole water chestnuts, drained and quartered

1 medium green bell pepper, cored and diced

1 medium red bell pepper, cored and diced

½ cup whole almonds, blanched or natural, toasted in 350°F oven until fragrant and golden

1 In a medium bowl, whisk together the cornstarch, wine, and ½ teaspoon salt. Add the chicken and mix well.

2 In a wok or stir-fry pan, heat the oil over high heat. Add the ginger and stir, until the oil is hot and the ginger sizzles. Stir up the chicken mixture and add it to the pan. Cook, stirring constantly, until the chicken turns white, 1 to 2 minutes.

3 Add the bamboo shoots, water chestnuts, and peppers and cook, stirring, until the peppers are tender-crisp and the chicken is cooked through, about 1 minute. Add the remaining ½ teaspoon salt and almonds and mix thoroughly. Remove and discard the ginger, if desired. Serve immediately.

➥ **VARIATION:** To give the dish a slightly sweet taste, add 1 to 1½ tablespoons hoisin sauce when adding the vegetables and reduce the salt to ½ teaspoon.

braised party wings

The first and second sections of a chicken wing, the drumette and wingette, are collectively called "party wings." If using whole chicken wings, cut them apart at the joints into three pieces. Discard the wing tips. These wings are delicious hot or cold.

✳ **SERVES 4 AS APPETIZERS**

---

2 pounds chicken party wings, about 18 to 20 pieces or 2½ pounds whole chicken wings

3 tablespoons oyster sauce

1 tablespoon light soy sauce

1 teaspoon Chinese rice wine or dry sherry

1 teaspoon sugar

½ teaspoon grated peeled fresh ginger

¼ cup canola oil

1 Rinse the wings, drain, and pat dry. In a small bowl, stir together the oyster sauce, soy sauce, wine, sugar, and ginger.

2 In a wok or stir-fry pan, heat the oil over medium-high heat until hot but not smoking. Test by dipping a wing into the oil; it should sizzle. Add half of the wings to the pan, spread in a single layer, and cook, turning occasionally for even browning, until lightly browned, 6 to 8 minutes. Remove, drain on paper towels, and brown the remaining wings in the same pan.

3 Drain the oil from the pan and wipe with a paper towel. Return the wings to the same pan over medium high heat. Add the oyster sauce mixture and ¼ cup water, stir, and bring to a boil. Reduce the heat to medium low until the liquid simmers; cover and continue cooking, stirring once or twice, until the wings are cooked through, about 10 minutes.

4 Uncover the pan, increase the heat to high, and bring the liquid to a boil. Stir constantly until the liquid is reduced and the wings are nicely glazed, about 2 minutes. Transfer the wings to a platter and serve hot or cold.

pork

kan shao green beans with pork

Kan shao, which means "dry cook," is a Sichuan style of cooking in which the ingredients are stir-fried over high heat until the liquid has completely reduced. The result is a truly rich and savory dish since the ingredients absorb all of the flavors.

✳ SERVES 4

1 pound green or wax beans, ends snapped off and strings removed

1 tablespoon Chinese rice wine or dry sherry

1 teaspoon cornstarch

4 ounces ground pork (½ cup)

3 tablespoons fermented black beans, coarsely chopped

1 tablespoon minced peeled fresh ginger

2 garlic cloves, minced

1 teaspoon crushed red pepper, or to taste

3 tablespoons dark soy sauce

1 teaspoon sugar

3 tablespoons canola oil

1 Snap the beans into 2-inch lengths. Rinse in cold water and drain thoroughly.

2 In a medium bowl, whisk together the wine and cornstarch. Add the pork and mix well.

3 In a small bowl, stir together the black beans, ginger, garlic, and crushed red pepper. In another small bowl, whisk together the soy sauce and ½ cup water.

4 In a wok or stir-fry pan, heat the oil over medium-high heat. Add the black bean mixture and stir a few times until aromatic. Stir up the pork mixture and add it to the pan. Turn the heat to high and cook, stirring, until the pork is no longer pink and separates, about 2 minutes.

5 Add the green beans and the soy sauce mixture. Stir a few times and then reduce the heat to medium. Cook, covered, for 5 minutes. Remove the lid and raise the heat to high. Stir constantly until the liquid is almost gone, about 5 minutes more. Serve immediately.

stir-fried pork with asparagus

I keep a few individually wrapped boneless pork chops in the freezer for easy last-minute stir-fry dishes like this one. Hoisin sauce lends a delicate sweetness to the dish, which enhances the natural goodness of fresh asparagus. ✳ **SERVES 3 TO 4**

---

1 pound asparagus

2 teaspoons cornstarch

1 teaspoon Chinese rice wine
or dry sherry

½ pound boneless pork chops

1 tablespoon dark soy sauce

2 tablespoons hoisin sauce

1 teaspoon sugar

3 tablespoons canola oil

1 garlic clove, sliced

1 Snap or cut off the tough ends of the asparagus, and if desired, strip off the small leaves on the spear up to 2 inches from the tip. Cut on the diagonal into 2-inch lengths.

2 In a medium bowl, whisk together the cornstarch and wine. Cut the pork into ¼-inch-thick strips the same length as the asparagus. Add to the cornstarch mixture and mix well. In a small bowl, whisk together the soy sauce, hoisin sauce, and sugar.

3 In a wok or stir-fry pan, heat 1 tablespoon of the oil over high heat until hot but not smoking. Test by dipping a piece of asparagus into the oil; it should sizzle. Add the asparagus and stir just until they turn a darker green, about 30 seconds. Add ¼ cup water, cover the pan, and cook over medium heat, stirring occasionally, until tender, 3 to 5 minutes, depending upon the thickness of the spears. Transfer the asparagus and any liquid to a platter.

4 Add the remaining 2 tablespoons of oil to the same pan and heat over high heat. Add the garlic and stir until the oil is hot and the garlic sizzles. Stir up the pork mixture, add to the pan, and cook, stirring constantly, until the pork is no longer pink, 2 to 3 minutes. Add the soy sauce mixture and stir for about 20 seconds. Return the asparagus to the pan and stir for another 30 seconds or so, until well mixed. Serve immediately.

bean sprouts with shredded pork and garlic chives

Garlic chives, also known as Chinese chives, have a deep garlic flavor. They are an easy-to-grow perennial, so they'll come back year after year. Be sure to give them plenty of room since you need to use a whole bunch at a time. ✳ **SERVES 4**

½ **pound thin-cut boneless pork chops**

2 **teaspoons Chinese rice wine or dry sherry**

2 **teaspoons cornstarch**

½ **teaspoon sugar**

3 **tablespoons light soy sauce**

¼ **pound garlic chives**

3 **tablespoons canola oil**

2 **slices unpeeled fresh ginger**

¾ **pound bean sprouts (about 4 heaping cups)**

1 Trim the fat from the pork chops. With the knife horizontal to the cutting board, split each chop into two flat pieces. With the pieces stacked together, cut the meat into ⅛-inch shreds.

2 In a medium bowl, whisk together the wine, cornstarch, sugar, and soy sauce. Add the pork and mix well.

3 Trim off and discard the white ends of the chives. Cut the leaves into 1-inch lengths.

4 In a wok or stir-fry pan, heat the oil over high heat. Add the ginger and stir until the oil is hot and the ginger sizzles. Stir up the pork mixture and add it to the pan. Cook, stirring constantly, until the pork pieces are separated and no longer pink, about 2 minutes.

5 Add the chives and the bean sprouts and cook, stirring, until the sprouts wilt, 2 to 3 minutes. Remove and discard the ginger, if desired. Serve immediately.

pork shreds with bean thread noodles and napa cabbage

Bean thread noodles, made from mung beans, are also known as cellophane noodles because when they are cooked they become transparent. Bean thread noodles have no flavor, but they soak up the flavors of the other ingredients. Be careful not to over-cook the noodles and be sure to serve the dish as soon as it is ready, or the noodles will become very soft and sticky. ✳ **SERVES 3 TO 4**

---

1 teaspoon cornstarch

3 tablespoons light soy sauce

1 teaspoon Chinese rice wine or dry sherry

½ pound lean boneless pork loin or boneless pork chop, shredded (about 1 cup)

4 ounces bean thread noodles

½ pound napa cabbage

3 tablespoons canola oil

1 slice unpeeled fresh ginger

⅓ cup thinly sliced scallions

½ cup canned chicken broth

1 In a medium bowl, whisk together the cornstarch, soy sauce, and wine. Add the pork and mix well.

2 Soak the bean thread noodles in hot (not boiling) water until soft. Drain carefully, keeping the strands together, and cut into 6-inch lengths with scissors. Wash the cabbage leaves thoroughly, drain, and cut into 1½-inch chunks. You should have about 4 cups.

3 In a wok or stir-fry pan, heat the oil over high heat. Add the ginger and stir until the oil is hot and the ginger sizzles. Add the scallions and stir for about 15 seconds. Stir up the pork mixture and add it to the pan, stirring constantly for about 1 minute. Add the cabbage and stir for 1 minute.

4 Add the broth to the pan, stir to mix, and cover. Let steam for about 4 minutes. Uncover, reduce the heat to medium, and stir in the softened bean thread noodles. Cook, stirring, until the noodles become transparent and the pork is no longer pink, about 2 minutes. Serve immediately.

moo shi pork

Moo Shi Pork (also known as Moo Shu) is served with Mandarin pancakes, sometimes called "doilies" because of their delicate texture. You can purchase the pancakes frozen in Asian markets. You can also eat Moo Shi Pork in an unconventional (but equally good) manner over steamed rice. ✳ **SERVES 4, OR ENOUGH TO FILL ABOUT 12 PANCAKES**

---

3 tablespoons dried wood ears

¼ cup dried golden needles (about ½ ounce)

1 teaspoon Chinese rice wine or dry sherry

3 tablespoons light soy sauce

1 teaspoon cornstarch

¼ pound lean boneless pork loin or boneless pork chop, shredded (about ½ cup)

4 tablespoons canola oil

2 large eggs, beaten

2 slices unpeeled fresh ginger

1½ cups shredded green cabbage (about 5 ounces)

1 cup sliced white mushrooms

6 ounces bean sprouts (about 2 cups)

2 scallions, bulbs split in half and cut into 1-inch pieces

1 Soak the wood ears and golden needles separately in hot water for 15 minutes, or until soft. Squeeze out the water, clean, rinse, and drain. Remove any tough parts and chop the wood ears coarsely into pieces about ½ inch in size. Cut off the stems of the golden needles if they are tough, and cut in half.

2 In a medium bowl, whisk together the wine, soy sauce, and cornstarch. Add the pork and mix well.

3 In a wok or stir-fry pan, heat 2 tablespoons of the oil over medium-high heat until the oil is hot, but not smoking. Add the eggs and scramble into fine pieces. Remove the eggs from the pan.

4 Add the remaining 2 tablespoons of oil to the same pan and heat over high heat. Add the ginger and stir until the oil is hot and the ginger sizzles. Stir up the pork mixture and add to the pan. Add the cabbage and 2 tablespoons water. Cook, stirring, until the pork loses its pink color and the cabbage just begins to wilt, about 2 minutes. Add the white mushrooms, bean sprouts, scallions, wood ears, and golden needles and stir constantly until the fresh vegetables are tender and the pork is no longer pink, about 1 minute more.

5 Return the eggs to the pan and stir until well mixed. Taste for salt. Remove and discard the ginger, if desired.

1½ teaspoons salt, or to taste

10 to 12 Mandarin pancakes (about 1 package), for serving

¾ cup hoisin sauce, for serving

6 To serve, first steam the pancakes in a steamer basket over simmering water until hot. Spread hoisin sauce on each pancake and place 3 or 4 tablespoons of Moo Shi in a strip down the middle. Don't overfill or it will be impossible to eat neatly. Roll up the pancakes and eat.

spicy chungking pork

This is a classic Sichuan dish named after Chongqing, a major city in Sichuan province. It is also known as "twice-cooked pork," because the pork is first poached and then stir-fried. I have simplified the recipe, without sacrificing flavor, by eliminating the first cooking. ✳ **SERVES 3 TO 4**

¾ **pound pork tenderloin**

2 teaspoons Chinese rice wine or dry sherry

4 teaspoons cornstarch

2 tablespoons fermented black beans, coarsely chopped

1 teaspoon crushed red pepper, or to taste

3 tablespoons hoisin sauce

2 teaspoons dark soy sauce

4 tablespoons canola oil

½ **pound green cabbage, cut in 1½-inch chunks (about 3 cups)**

1 medium red bell pepper, cored and cut into 1½-inch chunks

3 slices unpeeled fresh ginger

2 garlic cloves, crushed with the side of a knife and peeled

1 Slice the tenderloin crosswise ⅛ inch thick. (If necessary, freeze briefly first to make slicing easier.) In a medium bowl, whisk together the wine and 2 teaspoons of the cornstarch. Add the pork and mix well. In a small bowl, whisk the remaining cornstarch in ¼ cup water, making sure it is completely dissolved.

2 In another small bowl, stir together the black beans and crushed red pepper. In another small bowl, stir together the hoisin sauce and soy sauce.

3 In a wok or stir-fry pan, heat 2 tablespoons of the oil over high heat until hot but not smoking. Add the cabbage; it should sizzle. Cook, stirring, for about 3 minutes. Add the red bell pepper and cook for 2 minutes more. The cabbage may brown slightly. Remove to a plate.

4 Add the remaining 2 tablespoons of oil to the same pan and heat over high heat. Add the ginger and garlic and stir until the oil is hot and the ginger and garlic sizzle. Do not brown. Stir up the pork mixture, add to the pan, and cook, stirring briskly, until the pork is no longer pink, 2 to 3 minutes.

5 Add the black bean mixture and stir a few times. Stir up the sauce mixture, and add to the pan, mixing well. Return the vegetables to the pan, stir, then add the cornstarch mixture, and stir for 30 seconds. Remove and discard the ginger and garlic, if desired. Serve immediately.

yu xiang eggplant with pork

Although this dish contains no fish, the eggplant is cooked in the same type of flavorings that are used in the highly savory *yu xiang*, or "fragrant fish sauce" of Sichuan province. This dish contains very little meat, and you can make it without any meat at all if you like. If your eggplant is Asian or garden-fresh, leave the skin on for added texture, otherwise peel it entirely or peel it in alternating strips. Omit the crushed red pepper for a less spicy version. ✳ **SERVES 3 TO 4**

---

1 to 1¼ pounds eggplant, Asian or regular

1 teaspoon salt

3 tablespoons thinly sliced scallions, plus additional for garnish

1 tablespoon minced peeled fresh ginger

1 teaspoon minced garlic

1 to 3 teaspoons crushed red pepper, or to taste

1 tablespoon Sichuan hot bean sauce

1 tablespoon cider vinegar

1 teaspoon sugar

1 tablespoon dark soy sauce

1 tablespoon Chinese rice wine or dry sherry

1 Wash the eggplant and trim off the stem. Leave the skin on if eggplant is Asian or very fresh and the skin tender. Otherwise, peel completely or in alternating strips. Quarter the eggplant lengthwise (or cut into eighths if large) and cut again into bite-size pieces. Place in a colander, sprinkle with salt, toss, and let stand for 20 minutes. Rinse, drain, and pat dry. If using Asian eggplant, cut into bite-size pieces. It is not necessary to salt or rinse Asian eggplant.

2 In a small dish, mix together 3 tablespoons of scallions, the ginger, garlic, and crushed red pepper. In another small dish, combine the hot bean sauce, vinegar, sugar, and soy sauce. In a medium bowl, whisk together the wine and 1 teaspoon cornstarch. Add the pork and mix well.

3 In a wok or stir-fry pan, heat the oil over high heat until hot but not smoking. Test by dipping a piece of eggplant into the oil; it should sizzle. Stir the eggplant into the hot oil. The eggplant will initially absorb all the oil but will release it as it cooks. Do not add more oil. Cook, stirring and pressing the eggplant against the bottom of the pan with the back of a spatula, until it is soft and turns dark, about 6 minutes. Stir up the pork mixture, add it to the pan, and cook, stirring, until the pork is no longer pink and separates. Add the scallion mixture and stir for 1 minute.

(continued on page 56)

1 teaspoon cornstarch, plus 2 teaspoons dissolved in 1 tablespoon water

3 ounces ground lean pork (about ⅓ cup)

3 tablespoons canola oil

4 Add the bean sauce mixture and 1 cup water and stir to mix. Cover the pan, reduce the heat to medium, and simmer, stirring occasionally, until tender, 2 to 3 minutes. Remove the cover and thicken the sauce with the cornstarch mixture. Transfer to a shallow platter and sprinkle with thinly sliced scallions. Serve immediately.

sweet-and-sour pork northern style

This traditional northern Chinese version of sweet-and-sour pork does not require the batter or double deep-frying of the Americanized Cantonese style. Here I've given a recipe for the familiar sweet-and-sour sauce made red with ketchup and served with the lighter and easier to make northern-style pork nuggets. ✳ **SERVES 3 TO 4**

---

1 pound lean boneless pork loin

¼ teaspoon freshly ground black pepper

1 large egg

1 tablespoon light soy sauce

3 tablespoons cornstarch

⅓ cup white or cider vinegar

⅓ cup sugar

⅓ cup water

2½ tablespoons ketchup

¼ teaspoon salt

1 cup canola oil, for frying plus 1 tablespoon (optional)

1 tablespoon and 2 teaspoons cornstarch dissolved in 3 tablespoons water

1 cup canned pineapple chunks, drained

1 Cut the pork into ¾-inch cubes and toss with the pepper. In a medium bowl, whisk together the egg, soy sauce, and 3 tablespoons cornstarch. Add the pork and mix well. Let stand for 10 minutes.

2 In a saucepan, whisk together the vinegar, sugar, water, ketchup, and salt. Set aside on an unlit burner.

3 In a wok or stir-fry pan, heat the 1 cup of oil over high heat until the oil registers 350°F on a deep-fry or candy thermometer. Gently drop half of the pork, 1 piece at a time, into the hot oil and fry until light brown and crisp, about 6 minutes. Stir gently so all sides brown and the pieces don't stick together. Remove the pork from the oil with a wire strainer or slotted spoon and spread out on paper towels. Keep warm in a low oven. Bring the oil back to 350°F and fry the remaining pieces the same way.

4 Heat the sauce over medium heat. When sauce boils, stir in the cornstarch mixture. Continue stirring until the sauce thickens and turns translucent. If desired, add the additional tablespoon of oil to give the sauce a shine. Stir thoroughly. Add the pineapple and heat just until warm. Transfer the pork to a platter and cover with the hot sauce. Serve immediately.

sparerib nuggets in black bean sauce

Most people think of spareribs as something that calls for two-fisted eating, but the Chinese don't usually serve such large pieces of meat. They cut the ribs into small portions that can be handled with chopsticks. Ask your butcher to cut across the bones into 1-inch strips. You can then cut them apart through the meat into separate little pieces at home. ✳ **SERVES 3 TO 4**

---

3 tablespoons fermented black beans, coarsely chopped

1 tablespoon Chinese rice wine or dry sherry

2 teaspoons sugar

2 tablespoons light soy sauce

2 teaspoons minced garlic

1 teaspoon crushed red pepper (optional)

1 tablespoon canola oil

1½ pounds pork spareribs, trimmed, cut into 1-inch lengths, and ribs separated

1½ teaspoons cornstarch dissolved in 1 tablespoon water

1 In a small bowl, mix together the black beans with the wine, sugar, soy sauce, garlic, crushed red pepper, if using, and ¾ cup water.

2 In a wok or stir-fry pan, heat the oil over high heat until hot but not smoking. Test by dipping a sparerib into the oil; it should sizzle. Add the spareribs to the hot oil and brown for 4 to 5 minutes. Stir in the black bean mixture, cover, and cook over medium-low heat, stirring occasionally, until ribs are cooked, 20 to 25 minutes. Test by taking out a thick piece of rib and cutting through the meat. If meat is pink, continue cooking until it tests done.

3 Remove the cover and turn the heat up to medium-high. When the sauce boils, add the cornstarch mixture, and stir until thickened. Serve immediately.

beef

sliced beef with assorted vegetables

This is a good dish to make when your vegetable drawer holds small amounts of many different vegetables. I've given specific proportions in this recipe, but they can vary, according to what you have on hand. Add them one at a time, starting with the vegetables that take longer to cook. ✳ **SERVES 4 TO 5**

1 pound flank steak, trimmed

4 tablespoons dark soy sauce

1 tablespoon cornstarch

1 tablespoon Chinese rice wine or dry sherry

1 teaspoon sugar

3 tablespoons canola oil

2 cups broccoli florets

1 cup cauliflower florets

½ cup sliced carrots

1 cup red bell pepper chunks

1 cup sliced celery

1 (8-ounce) can sliced water chestnuts, drained

2 slices unpeeled fresh ginger

1 garlic clove, crushed with the side of a knife and peeled

1 tablespoon fermented black beans, coarsely chopped (optional)

Salt, to taste

1 With your knife vertical to the cutting board, slice the steak with the grain along the full length of the meat into long strips about 2 inches wide. Then slice the long pieces against the grain into ⅛-inch thick slices. In a medium bowl, whisk together the soy sauce, cornstarch, wine, and sugar. Add the beef and mix well.

2 In a wok or stir-fry pan, heat 1 tablespoon of the oil over high heat until hot but not smoking. Test by dipping a vegetable into the oil; it should sizzle. Add the broccoli, cauliflower, and carrots and cook, stirring, for 1 minute. Add ¼ cup water, reduce the heat to medium, stir a few times, cover, and cook for 2 minutes. Add the pepper, celery, and water chestnuts and cook, stirring, until tender-crisp, about 2 minutes more. Transfer the vegetables to a shallow platter.

3 Add the remaining 2 tablespoons of oil to the same pan. Add the ginger and garlic and stir until the oil is hot and the ginger and garlic sizzle. Stir up the beef mixture and add it to the pan. Cook, stirring constantly, until the beef is almost cooked, about 2 minutes. Add ¼ cup water and the black beans, if using. Stir to mix and return the vegetables to the pan. Taste and add salt as needed. Stir thoroughly. Remove and discard the garlic, if desired. Serve immediately.

➤➤ **NOTE:** If the sauce seems thinner than you'd like (some vegetables release more liquid than others), thicken with 1 teaspoon cornstarch dissolved in 1 tablespoon water.

stir-fried broccoli beef
in oyster sauce

Chinese restaurants often serve this over a bed of freshly steamed rice as a one-dish meal for people who want a quick lunch or snack. ✳ **SERVES 3 TO 4**

---

1 pound flank steak, trimmed

1 tablespoon dark soy sauce

1 tablespoon cornstarch

1 tablespoon Chinese rice wine or dry sherry

1 teaspoon sugar

1 pound broccoli

3 tablespoons canola oil

¼ cup canned chicken broth or water

2 slices unpeeled fresh ginger

1 garlic clove, crushed with the side of a knife and peeled

½ cup canned sliced bamboo shoots, drained

4 tablespoons oyster sauce

1 Slice the steak with the grain into long strips about 2 inches wide. Then slice the long pieces against the grain into ⅛-inch thick slices. In a medium bowl, whisk together the soy sauce, cornstarch, wine, and sugar. Add the beef and mix well.

2 Trim and peel the broccoli stalks. Chop the flower heads from the stalks and cut into florets. Slice the peeled stalks into bite-size pieces.

3 In a wok or stir-fry pan, heat 1 tablespoon of the oil over high heat until the oil is hot but not smoking. Test by dipping a piece of broccoli into the oil; it should sizzle. Add the broccoli and stir constantly for about 30 seconds. Stir in the broth, reduce the heat to medium, and cover the pan. Continue cooking, stirring occasionally, for another minute or two until broccoli is tender-crisp. Remove from the pan and spread out on a plate. Do not pile into a bowl, as the heat generated by the broccoli will overcook the pieces on the bottom.

4 With the heat still on high, add the remaining 2 tablespoons of oil to the same pan. Add the ginger and garlic and stir until the oil is hot and the ginger and garlic sizzle. Stir up the beef mixture and add to the pan. Cook, stirring, until the meat is almost done, about 2 minutes. Add the bamboo shoots and oyster sauce and continue stirring until the beef is cooked, about 1 minute more. Return the broccoli and mix thoroughly. Remove and discard the ginger and garlic, if desired. Serve immediately.

stir-fried beef with asparagus

My mother taught me to remove the small lower leaves that look like scales on the asparagus spear for a neater appearance and to get rid of any lingering sand or grit. The very first time I saw an asparagus plant was at the Greenough farm in Massachusetts. When I was young we used to have annual picnics there with the Greenough family and their guests. I remember meeting Beverly Sills, a family member who had not yet been discovered by the general public, and the wonderful composer and musician Daniel Pinkham. My mother was particularly thrilled with the fresh vegetables. We would go into the fields and pick our own vegetables for lunch. ✳ **SERVES 3 TO 4**

---

1 pound flank steak, trimmed

2 teaspoons cornstarch

1 tablespoon Chinese rice wine or dry sherry

2 tablespoons dark soy sauce

½ teaspoon sugar

1 pound asparagus

3 tablespoons canola oil

1 slice unpeeled fresh ginger

1 large onion, sliced ½ inch thick (about 1 cup)

1 Slice the steak along the grain the full length of the meat into long strips about 2 inches wide. Then slice the long pieces against the grain into ⅛-inch thick slices. In a medium bowl, whisk together the cornstarch, wine, soy sauce, and sugar. Add the beef and mix well.

2 Snap or cut off the tough ends of the asparagus and if desired, strip off the small leaves on the spear up to 2 inches from the tip. Cut each spear on the diagonal into 2-inch pieces.

3 In a wok or stir-fry pan, heat 1 tablespoon of the oil over high heat until hot but not smoking. Test by dipping a piece of asparagus into the oil; it should sizzle. Add the asparagus and stir for about 30 seconds. Add ¼ cup water and stir briefly. Cook, covered, just until the vegetables are tender-crisp, 1 to 2 minutes. Transfer the asparagus to a platter.

4 Put the remaining 2 tablespoons of oil into the same pan, add the ginger and stir until the ginger begins to sizzle. Add the onion and cook, stirring constantly, until wilted but not browned, about 1 minute. Stir up the beef mixture and add it to the pan. Cook, stirring constantly, until the beef is almost done, about 2 minutes. Return the asparagus to the pan and stir thoroughly until reheated. Remove and discard the ginger, if desired. Serve immediately.

beef with zucchini

At the end of the summer, when all of the gardeners you know are trying to give away their surplus zucchini, this stir-fried dish is not only delicious but also economical. This recipe works equally well with other types of summer squash such as yellow and pattypan squash. ✳ **SERVES 3 TO 4**

---

1 pound flank steak, trimmed

3 tablespoons dark soy sauce

1 tablespoon cornstarch

1 tablespoon Chinese rice wine or dry sherry

1 teaspoon sugar

3 tablespoons canola oil

1 slice unpeeled fresh ginger

1 garlic clove, crushed with the side of a knife and peeled

1 medium red onion, cut into chunks

3 small zucchini, sliced on the diagonal ¼ inch thick

½ teaspoon salt, or to taste

1 Slice the steak with the grain into 2-inch wide long strips. Then slice the strips against the grain into ⅛-inch thick slices. In a medium bowl, whisk together the soy sauce, cornstarch, wine, and sugar. Add the beef and mix well.

2 In a wok or stir-fry pan, heat the oil over high heat. Add the ginger and garlic and stir until the oil is hot and the ginger and garlic sizzle. Do not brown. Add the onion and cook, stirring constantly, for 1 minute. Stir up the beef mixture and add to the pan. Cook, stirring and adding water a tablespoon at a time as necessary to keep the meat from sticking to the pan, for another minute.

3 Add the zucchini and cook, stirring constantly, until just tender, about 2 minutes. Taste and add salt as needed. Remove and discard the ginger and garlic, if desired. Serve immediately.

dining car beef and red onions

During our first trip to China in 1972, my mother, my brother Stephen, and I had this dish many times as we went by train from Guangzhou (Canton) to Shanghai. As we traveled north, away from the areas of abundant produce, the train's cook would turn more and more to root vegetables, which keep well without refrigeration. You may substitute Spanish or Vidalia onions. ✳ **SERVES 3 TO 4**

---

1 pound flank steak, trimmed

1 tablespoon cornstarch

1 tablespoon Chinese rice wine or dry sherry

3 tablespoons dark soy sauce

1 teaspoon sugar

4 tablespoons canola oil

1 slice unpeeled fresh ginger

2 medium red onions, cut into 1-inch chunks

1 red bell pepper, cored and cut into 1-inch chunks

¼ cup canned chicken broth or water (optional)

1 Slice the steak with the grain into 2-inch-wide long strips. Then slice the long strips against the grain into ⅛-inch-thick slices. In a medium bowl, whisk together the cornstarch, wine, soy sauce, and sugar. Add the beef and mix well.

2 In a wok or stir-fry pan, heat 2 tablespoons of the oil over high heat. Add the ginger and stir until the oil is hot and the ginger sizzles. Add the onions and stir for about 30 seconds. Add the pepper and cook, stirring constantly, until the vegetables are tender-crisp, about 30 seconds. Remove from the pan and spread out on a plate.

3 Add the remaining 2 tablespoons of oil to the same pan. When it is hot, stir up the beef mixture and add it to the pan. Cook, stirring constantly, adding ¼ cup broth, if using, for more gravy and to keep the meat from sticking to the pan, for about 2 minutes. Return the vegetables to the pan and stir for about 30 seconds to mix. Remove and discard the ginger, if desired. Serve immediately with hot steamed rice.

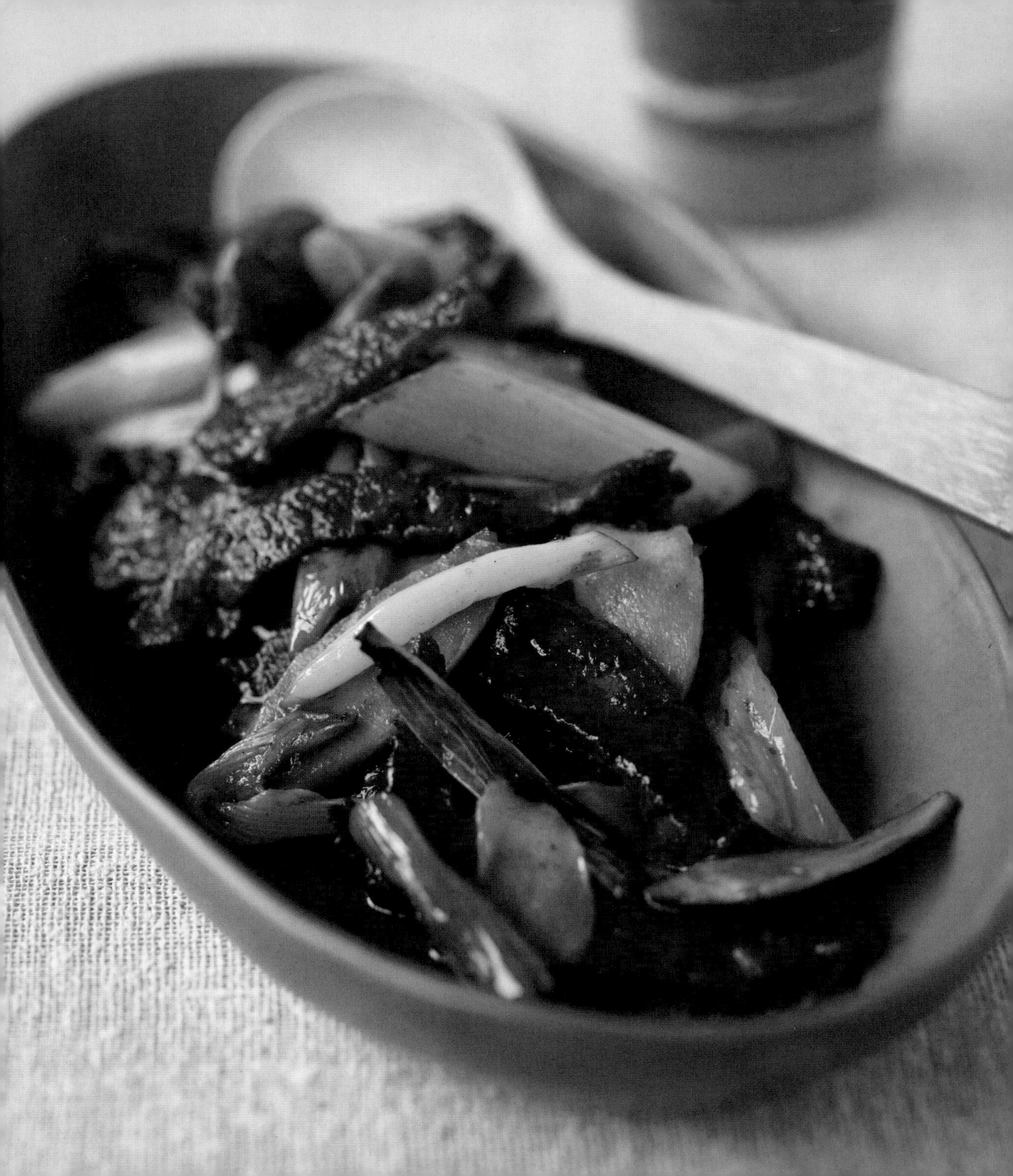

beef with scallions and bamboo shoots

Scallions or green onions are favorite aromatic ingredients for Chinese cooking. Here, they are used as one of the main ingredients. ✳ **SERVES 3 TO 4**

---

1 pound flank steak, trimmed

2 tablespoons hoisin sauce

2 tablespoons dark soy sauce

1 tablespoon cornstarch

1 tablespoon Chinese rice wine or dry sherry

1 teaspoon sugar

3 tablespoons canola oil

2 sliced unpeeled fresh ginger

1 garlic clove, crushed with the side of a knife and peeled

¼ cup canned chicken broth or water

1 (8-ounce) can sliced bamboo shoots, drained

5 scallions, bulbs split and cut into 2-inch pieces

1 teaspoon sesame oil

1 Slice the beef with the grain along the full length of the meat into long strips about 2 inches wide. Then slice the long pieces against the grain into ⅛-inch-thick slices. In a medium bowl, whisk together the hoisin sauce, soy sauce, cornstarch, wine, and sugar. Add the beef and mix well.

2 In a wok or stir-fry pan, heat the oil over medium-high heat. Add the ginger and garlic and stir until the oil is hot and the ginger and garlic sizzle. Do not brown. Stir up the beef mixture and add it to the pan. Stir thoroughly for about 1 minute until the beef begins to change color and separate.

3 Stir in the broth, add the bamboo shoots and cook, stirring constantly, until the beef is almost cooked, 1 to 2 minutes. Add the scallions and cook, stirring, until the scallions are wilted and the beef is fully cooked, 1 to 2 minutes more. Drizzle with the sesame oil and mix well. Remove and discard the ginger and garlic, if desired. Serve immediately.

spicy beef shreds with carrots and celery

The traditional method of preparing this Sichuan dish is to deep-fry the shredded beef in oil first. Shredding the meat with the grain gives it a chewy texture and frying makes it dry and crisp. I have adapted the recipe to use a stir-fry method, which is faster and lower in fat—and every bit as delicious. ✳ **SERVES 3 TO 4**

---

1 pound flank streak, trimmed

2 tablespoons dark soy sauce

1 teaspoon Chinese rice wine or dry sherry

2 teaspoons grated peeled fresh ginger

4 tablespoons canola oil

1½ cups shredded carrots (about 3 medium)

2 cups shredded celery (about 4 stalks)

1 to 3 teaspoons crushed red pepper, or to taste

½ teaspoon salt, or to taste

1 teaspoon cornstarch dissolved in 1 tablespoon water

1 Slice the steak against the grain into 2-inch-wide pieces. With the knife horizontal to the cutting board, split the meat into three or four pieces. Pile up the pieces and cut the meat into ⅛-inch shreds with the grain of the meat. In a medium bowl, whisk together the soy sauce, wine, and ginger. Add the beef shreds and mix well.

2 In a wok or stir-fry pan, heat the oil over high heat until hot, but not smoking. Test by dipping the spatula into the beef mixture and then into the oil; it should sizzle. Stir up the beef mixture and add it to the pan. Cook, stirring briskly, until the shreds separate and are no longer pink, about 2 minutes. Remove the beef with a wire strainer or slotted spoon to a plate, leaving the liquid in the pan.

3 Return the pan to high heat, add the carrots, and cook for 30 seconds. Add the celery and crushed red pepper and stir for 1 minute. Return the beef to the pan and stir a few times. Taste the sauce and add salt as needed. Add the cornstarch mixture and stir until thickened. Serve immediately.

orange peel beef

Instead of the traditional dried tangerine peels, I like the convenience of using fresh orange zest. Blanching the zest in boiling water reduces its bitterness.

✳ **SERVES 3 TO 4**

---

1 pound flank steak, trimmed

3 tablespoons light soy sauce

1 tablespoon plus 2 teaspoons Chinese rice wine or dry sherry

1 tablespoon cornstarch

½ cup plus 1 tablespoon canola oil

2 teaspoons sugar

¼ cup canned chicken broth

¼ cup thinly shredded orange zest (avoid white pith)

2 tablespoons minced peeled fresh ginger

1 tablespoon minced garlic

2 scallions, bulbs split and cut on the diagonal into 1-inch pieces

6 dried whole chile peppers, seeded

1 Slice the steak lengthwise with the grain into 2-inch wide strips. Then slice the long strips against the grain into ⅛-inch-thick slices. In a medium bowl, whisk together 1 tablespoon of the soy sauce, 2 teaspoons of the wine, and the cornstarch. Add the beef, mix well, and stir in 1 tablespoon of the oil. Let stand for 10 minutes. In a small bowl, whisk together the remaining 2 tablespoons soy sauce and remaining 1 tablespoon wine, the sugar, and broth.

2 Bring 4 cups water to a boil in a small saucepan. Add the orange zest and boil for 3 to 4 minutes. Drain, rinse in cold water, and shake dry.

3 In a wok or stir-fry pan, heat the remaining ½ cup oil over high heat until hot but not smoking. Test by dipping the spatula into the beef mixture and then into the oil; it should sizzle. Stir up the beef mixture and cook, stirring with chopsticks to separate the pieces of meat, until no longer pink, about 2 minutes. Remove the meat with a wire strainer or slotted spoon to a colander placed over a heatproof bowl and let drain.

4 Remove all but 2 tablespoons of the oil from the pan and return to the heat. Add the orange zest, ginger, garlic, scallions, and chiles. Stir over high heat for about 1 minute or until the garlic begins to color; don't allow the garlic to burn or it will become bitter. Return the beef to the pan, pour in the sauce, and cook, stirring, until the liquid is almost gone, about 3 minutes more. Transfer to a platter and serve immediately.

beef with mixed sweet peppers

I like the colorful contrast that red, green, and yellow bell peppers give to this dish, but if you are unable to get red or yellow peppers, it is fine to substitute all green ones. ✳ **SERVES 3 TO 4**

---

1 pound flank steak, trimmed
3 tablespoons dark soy sauce

1 tablespoon cornstarch

1 tablespoon Chinese rice wine or dry sherry

1 teaspoon sugar

4 tablespoons canola oil

1 green pepper, cored and cut into 1-inch chunks

1 red bell pepper, cored and cut into 1-inch chunks

1 yellow bell pepper, cored and cut into 1-inch chunks

1 slice unpeeled fresh ginger

1 (8-ounce) can sliced bamboo shoots, drained

½ teaspoon salt, or to taste

1 Slice the steak along the grain into 2-inch wide strips. Then slice the strips against the grain into ⅛-inch thick slices. In a medium bowl, whisk together the soy sauce, cornstarch, wine, and sugar. Add the beef and mix well.

2 In a wok or stir-fry pan, heat 2 tablespoons of the oil over high heat until hot. Test by dipping a spatula into the beef mixture and then into the oil; it should sizzle. Add the peppers and stir for 1 minute. Transfer to a platter.

3 Add the remaining 2 tablespoons oil to the same pan and heat over high heat. Add the ginger and stir until the oil is hot and the ginger sizzles. Stir up the beef mixture and add it to the pan. Cook, stirring constantly, until beef is almost done, about 2 minutes. Add the bamboo shoots and return the peppers to the pan and stir well for 30 seconds or more to reheat the vegetables. Taste and add salt as needed. Remove and discard the ginger, if desired. Serve immediately.

black pepper beef with green beans

A Cantonese favorite that uses freshly ground black pepper for spiciness, but this dish is not so much hot and spicy as deeply flavorful. Use more or less pepper to suit your taste. ✳ **SERVES 4**

---

1 pound green beans, ends snapped off and strings removed

¾ pound flank steak, trimmed

2 tablespoons dark soy sauce

1 tablespoon cornstarch

1 tablespoon Chinese rice wine or dry sherry

1 teaspoon sugar

2 teaspoons freshly ground black pepper, or to taste

3 tablespoons canola oil

2 slices unpeeled fresh ginger

1 cup sliced onion

1 Snap the green beans in half or thirds to make pieces about 2½ inches long. Rinse in cold water and drain thoroughly.

2 Slice the steak with the grain into 2-inch wide long strips. Then slice the strips against the grain into ⅛-inch thick slices. In a medium bowl, whisk together the soy sauce, cornstarch, wine, sugar, and black pepper. Add the beef and mix well.

3 In a wok or stir-fry pan, heat 1 tablespoon of the oil over high heat until the oil is hot, but not smoking. Test by dipping the spatula into the beef mixture and then into the oil; it should sizzle. Add the green beans and stir for about 1 minute. Add ¼ cup water and reduce the heat to medium. Cover and cook until tender-crisp, 6 to 9 minutes. Transfer the beans and any liquid to a shallow dish.

4 Add the remaining 2 tablespoons of oil to the same pan and raise the heat to high. Add the ginger and stir until the oil is hot and the ginger sizzles. Add the onion and stir constantly for 1 minute. Stir up the beef mixture and add it to the pan. Cook, stirring, until the beef is no longer pink, about 2 minutes.

5 Return the beans and any liquid to the pan and stir until thoroughly mixed and heated, about 30 seconds. Remove and discard the ginger, if desired, and serve immediately.

seafood

cantonese shrimp in lobster sauce

This has always been a favorite American-Chinese dish. There's actually no lobster in this dish at all. Rather, the shrimp is cooked in the type of sauce the Cantonese use for lobster. It's delicious served with lots of steaming, fresh-cooked rice. ✳ **SERVES 3 TO 4**

---

2 teaspoons Chinese rice wine or dry sherry

3 tablespoons cornstarch

1 pound medium or large shrimp, shelled and deveined

¼ pound ground lean pork (about ½ cup)

2 teaspoons dark soy sauce

¼ teaspoon sugar

3 tablespoons canola oil

2 slices unpeeled fresh ginger

2 garlic cloves, crushed with the side of a knife and peeled

2 tablespoons fermented black beans, minced

Salt, to taste

1 large egg, beaten

1 In a medium bowl, whisk together 1 teaspoon of the wine and 1 tablespoon of the cornstarch. Add the shrimp and mix well.

2 In a small bowl, whisk together the remaining 2 tablespoons of cornstarch with ¼ cup water, making sure it dissolves completely. In a medium bowl, mix together the pork, the remaining teaspoon of wine, the soy sauce, and sugar.

3 In a wok or stir-fry pan, heat the oil over medium high heat until hot but not smoking. Test by dipping the spatula into the shrimp mixture and then into the oil; it should sizzle. Stir up the shrimp mixture and add it to the pan, and cook, stirring constantly, until the shrimp turns opaque and pink, 1 to 2 minutes. Remove the shrimp from the pan with a slotted spoon, leaving as much oil as you can in the pan.

4 Add the ginger, garlic, and black beans to the same pan and stir a few times. Add the pork mixture and stir for about 30 seconds. Add 1 cup water, bring to a boil, cover, lower the heat to a simmer, and cook for 2 minutes. Taste and salt as needed.

5 Uncover and return the shrimp to the pan. Remove and discard the ginger and garlic, if desired. Add the cornstarch mixture and stir until thickened. Pour the beaten egg into the pan in a thin stream. Give 2 big stirs and serve immediately.

shanghainese shrimp with peas

Peas go nicely with shrimp, complementing but not overpowering them, and their bright green color is pretty against the pink of cooked shrimp. This is a perennial favorite at Shanghai restaurants. ✳ **SERVES 3 TO 4**

¼ **teaspoon grated peeled fresh ginger**

1 teaspoon Chinese rice wine or dry sherry

1 teaspoon cornstarch

1 teaspoon salt

1 pound medium shrimp, shelled and deveined

1 cup green peas, fresh or frozen and thawed

1 scallion, bulb split and cut into 2-inch pieces

3 tablespoons canola oil

1 In a medium bowl, whisk together the ginger, wine, cornstarch, and salt. Add the shrimp and mix well.

2 If using fresh peas, drop them in boiling water and cook for 1 minute. Drain immediately and run under cold water to stop the cooking.

3 In a wok or stir-fry pan, heat the oil over medium-high heat until the oil is hot but not smoking Test by dipping a scallion piece into the oil; it should sizzle. Add the scallions and stir a few times. Add the peas and stir for 1 minute. Stir up the shrimp mixture and add it to the pan. Cook, stirring, until the shrimp turn opaque and pink, about 1 minute more. Transfer the shrimp and peas to a platter. Remove and discard the scallions, if desired. Serve immediately.

shrimp with black beans

Seafood and fermented black beans are commonly combined in Cantonese-style dishes. It's amazing how everyday ingredients take on a whole new character with just a little of this extraordinary seasoning. This family-style dish is not usually served at banquets. It is not considered elegant enough because the dark sauce covers the coral-colored shrimp. At home it is enjoyed with great relish. ✳ **SERVES 3 TO 4**

---

1 teaspoon Chinese rice wine or dry sherry

1 teaspoon cornstarch

1 pound large shrimp, shelled and deveined

3 tablespoons canola oil

1 tablespoon thinly sliced scallions

1 tablespoon minced peeled fresh ginger

1 garlic clove, crushed with the side of a knife and peeled

3 tablespoons fermented black beans, coarsely chopped

Salt, to taste

1 In a medium bowl, whisk together the wine and cornstarch. Add the shrimp and mix well.

2 In a wok or stir-fry pan, heat the oil over high heat until hot but not smoking. Test by dipping the spatula into the shrimp mixture and then into the oil; it should sizzle. Add the scallions, ginger, garlic, and black beans and stir a few times. Mix up the shrimp mixture and add it to the pan. Add 2 tablespoons water and cook, stirring constantly, until the shrimp is opaque, about 2 minutes. Taste the sauce and add salt as needed. Serve immediately.

coral and jade

My mother coined this name for a popular shrimp dish that we served at our restaurant. The shrimp is stir-fried in a light tomato sauce, which accentuates the pink color of the cooked shrimp and makes it resemble coral. Snow peas when cooked take on the green color of imperial jade, so prized by the Chinese. What lovely imagery for a lovely dish! ✳ **SERVES 3 OR 4**

---

1 teaspoon grated peeled fresh ginger

1 teaspoon Chinese rice wine or dry sherry

1 teaspoon cornstarch

½ to 1 teaspoon salt or to taste

1 pound large or medium shrimp, shelled and deveined

3 tablespoons canola oil

¼ pound snow peas, ends snapped off and strings removed, cut in half on the diagonal

2 tablespoons ketchup

1 (8-ounce) can sliced water chestnuts, drained

1 In a medium bowl, whisk together the ginger, wine, cornstarch, and ¼ teaspoon salt. Add the shrimp and mix well.

2 In a wok or stir-fry pan, heat 1 tablespoon of the oil over medium heat until hot but not smoking. Test by dipping the end of a snow pea into the oil; it should sizzle. Add the snow peas and stir just until they turn a darker green, about 30 seconds. Do not scorch the tender snow peas inadvertently by heating the oil too hot. Remove the snow peas and spread out on a plate.

3 Add the remaining 2 tablespoons of oil to the same pan and heat over high heat. Stir up the shrimp mixture, add it to the pan, and cook, stirring constantly, until the shrimp turn opaque and pink, 1 to 2 minutes. Stir in the ketchup, water chestnuts, and ¼ teaspoon salt and stir-fry for about 30 seconds. Return the snow peas to the pan and mix together for 30 seconds to 1 minute. Remove from the heat and taste, adding more salt as needed. Transfer to a serving dish. Serve immediately.

sweet and sour shrimp

Most restaurant-style sweet-and-sour shrimp is coated in a thick batter, fried in lots of oil, and served in a cloying sauce. The shrimp here are lightly coated in a thin cornstarch paste, shallow-fried, and served in a light, tart sauce that does not overwhelm their delicate flavor. ✳ **SERVES 3 TO 4**

---

1 tablespoon Chinese rice wine or dry sherry

3 tablespoons light soy sauce

5 tablespoons cornstarch

½ teaspoon salt

1 pound large shrimp, shelled and deveined

1 medium red bell pepper, cored and cut into 1-inch cubes

1 medium green bell pepper, cored and cut into 1-inch cubes

1 cup canned pineapple chunks, well drained, syrup reserved

⅓ cup cider vinegar

⅓ cup plus 1 tablespoon sugar

¼ cup ketchup

1 garlic clove, crushed with the side of a knife and peeled

1 cup canola oil

1 In a medium bowl, whisk together the wine, 1 tablespoon of the soy sauce, 3 tablespoons of the cornstarch, and salt until you have a smooth paste. Add the shrimp and mix well. Let stand for 20 minutes.

2 Bring a small saucepan of water to boil and add the peppers. As soon as the water returns to a boil, drain immediately and run under cold water to stop the cooking. Add the pineapple to the peppers.

3 In a small bowl, combine the vinegar, sugar, ⅓ cup of reserved pineapple syrup, ketchup, and the remaining 2 tablespoons of soy sauce. In another small bowl, dissolve the remaining 2 tablespoons of cornstarch in ⅓ cup water.

4 In a wok or stir-fry pan, heat 1 cup of the oil over medium-high heat to 350°F to 375°F on a deep-fry or candy thermometer. Drop half of the shrimp, one at a time, into the pan. Cook, turning the shrimp carefully, until the shrimp turn pink and are lightly crisp, 2 to 3 minutes. Transfer to a dish lined with paper towels. Continue with the rest of the shrimp. Keep in a warm oven while you make the sauce.

5 Reserve 1 tablespoon of the oil and discard the rest. Wipe the pan clean with paper towels. Heat the reserved oil in the wok over medium heat. Add the garlic and stir until the garlic sizzles. Add the ketchup mixture to the pan and stir constantly, until the mixture comes to a boil. Stir in the cornstarch mixture and continue stirring until the sauce thickens and becomes translucent. Remove and discard the garlic Add the pineapple chunks, peppers, and shrimp. Mix well to coat the shrimp. Transfer to a platter and serve immediately.

crystal shrimp

There is no soy sauce to darken the clear white sauce in this Shanghai dish. That's why the shrimp are described as crystal. The original recipe calls for deep-frying the shrimp, but I prefer this version. ✳ **SERVES 3 TO 4**

---

1 teaspoon Chinese rice wine or dry sherry

1 teaspoon cornstarch

1 scant teaspoon salt

¼ teaspoon grated peeled fresh ginger

1 pound medium shrimp, shelled and deveined

1 scallion, bulb split, cut into 2-inch pieces

4 tablespoons canola oil

1 In a medium bowl, whisk together the wine, cornstarch, salt, and ginger. Add the shrimp and mix well, then mix in the scallions.

2 In a wok or stir-fry pan, heat the oil over high heat until hot but not smoking. Test by dipping the spatula into the shrimp mixture and then into the oil; it should sizzle. Stir up the shrimp mixture and add it to the pan. Cook, stirring briskly, until the shrimp turn opaque and pink, 1 to 2 minutes. Transfer the shrimp to a platter with a slotted spoon. Remove and discard the scallion, if desired. Serve immediately.

yangzhou slippery shrimp

Yangzhou, an ancient city located north of Shanghai, is known for its fine cuisine. I discovered this popular shrimp dish at a Yangzhou-style Chinese restaurant in Los Angeles. ✳ **SERVES 4**

---

1 pound extra-large shrimp, shelled and deveined (about 30)

5½ teaspoons cornstarch

⅛ teaspoon salt

1 teaspoon minced peeled fresh ginger

2 teaspoons finely minced garlic

1 tablespoon ketchup

1 tablespoon cider vinegar

1 tablespoon Chinese rice wine or dry sherry

1½ tablespoons sugar

½ cup canola oil

1 tablespoon thinly sliced scallion, green part only

1 In a medium bowl, mix the shrimp with 4 teaspoons of the cornstarch and the salt. In a small bowl, whisk together the remaining 1½ teaspoons cornstarch with 2 teaspoons water, making sure it completely dissolves.

2 In another small bowl, combine the ginger and garlic. In a third small bowl, whisk together the ketchup, vinegar, wine, sugar, and 2 tablespoons water.

3 In a wok or stir-fry pan, heat the oil over high heat until the oil is hot but not smoking. Test by dipping the spatula into the shrimp mixture and then into the oil; it should sizzle. Stir up the shrimp mixture and add it to the hot oil. Stir gently to keep the shrimp from sticking together. Cook until they turn opaque and pink, about 1 minute. Remove the shrimp from the oil with a wire strainer and drain on paper towels. Reserve 2 tablespoons of the oil and discard the rest. Wipe the pan clean with a paper towel.

4 Heat the reserved oil in the pan over medium-high heat and stir in the garlic and ginger. Add the ketchup mixture and stir a few times, then return the shrimp to the pan. Stir constantly until the liquid comes to a boil. Stir up the cornstarch mixture and add it to the pan and continue stirring until thickened. Sprinkle the scallions over the top and give two or three big stirs. Transfer to a platter and serve immediately.

shrimp in spicy tomato sauce

Although ketchup is a commonplace American staple, this sauce is anything but mundane. The combination of vinegar, ginger, and ketchup is sublime. ✳ **SERVES 3 TO 4**

---

1 tablespoon plus 2 teaspoons Chinese rice wine or dry sherry

1 tablespoon cider vinegar

4 tablespoons ketchup

1 teaspoon light or dark soy sauce

½ teaspoon salt

2 teaspoons sugar

1 teaspoon grated peeled fresh ginger plus 1 slice unpeeled ginger

2 teaspoons cornstarch

1 pound medium shrimp, shelled and deveined

3 tablespoons canola oil

2 garlic cloves, crushed with the side of a knife and peeled

3 tablespoons thinly sliced scallions

1 In a small bowl, stir together 1 tablespoon of the wine, the vinegar, ketchup, soy sauce, salt, sugar, and grated ginger.

2 In a medium bowl, whisk together the cornstarch and the remaining 2 teaspoons wine. Add the shrimp and mix well.

3 In a wok or stir-fry pan, heat the oil over high heat. Add the garlic and ginger slice and stir until the oil is hot and the garlic and ginger sizzle. Stir up the shrimp mixture and add it to the hot oil. Cook, stirring, until the shrimp turn opaque and pink, about 1 minute. Add the ketchup mixture to the pan and stir until evenly coated. Sprinkle the minced scallions over the shrimp, mix well, and transfer to a platter. Remove and discard the ginger slice and garlic, if desired. Serve immediately.

stir-fried fish fillets with vegetables

Use a firm whitefish for stir-frying and stir gently to avoid breaking up the pieces.

✳ SERVES 4

---

1 cup dried black mushrooms, softened in hot water for 15 minutes

1 cup snow peas, ends snapped off and strings removed

1 pound firm whitefish fillets, such as cod, haddock, mahi-mahi, carp, hake, or pollock

2 teaspoons Chinese rice wine or dry sherry

¼ teaspoon grated peeled fresh ginger plus 2 slices unpeeled fresh ginger

½ teaspoon salt, or to taste

5 tablespoons canola oil

1 garlic clove, crushed with the side of a knife and peeled

½ pound napa or Chinese celery cabbage, quartered lengthwise, cored, and cut into 1½-inch chunks

½ cup canned chicken broth

1 (8-ounce) can sliced bamboo shoots, drained

2 teaspoons cornstarch dissolved in 1 tablespoon water

1 Drain the mushrooms and squeeze dry. Cut off the stems with scissors and discard. Slice the caps in halves or quarters so the pieces are uniform in size. Cut the larger snow peas in half on the diagonal so the peas are of fairly uniform size.

2 Cut the fish into 2-inch-square pieces. In a medium bowl, combine the wine, grated ginger, and ½ teaspoon of the salt. Add the fish and mix well.

3 In a wok or stir-fry pan, heat 3 tablespoons of the oil over high heat until the oil is hot but not smoking. Test by dipping the spatula into the fish mixture and then into the oil; it should sizzle. Stir up the fish mixture and add to the hot oil. Stir gently for about 30 seconds, or until the fish is partially done. Remove to a platter.

4 Add the remaining 2 tablespoons of oil to the same pan and add the sliced ginger and garlic. Stir around the pan until they sizzle. Add the cabbage and broth, stir, and cook, covered, for about 1 minute. Remove the lid and add the mushrooms, snow peas, and bamboo shoots. Stir-fry until the snow peas turn bright green.

5 Return the fish to the pan and stir gently. Add the cornstarch mixture and stir gently until the sauce thickens. Taste and add additional salt, if needed. Remove and discard the ginger slices and garlic, if desired. Serve immediately.

clams in black bean sauce

The Chinese serve clams cooked in their shells on special occasions like the lunar New Year. They are considered symbolic of prosperity and wealth because when the clam shells open they resemble the shape of the silver ingots used in ancient China.

✳ SERVES 2

---

2 pounds littleneck or cherry-stone clams (about 12)

2 garlic cloves, crushed with the side of a knife and peeled

2 slices unpeeled fresh ginger

1 scallion, bulb split, cut into 1-inch lengths

3 tablespoons fermented black beans, coarsely chopped

1 fresh Thai chile, thinly sliced (optional)

2 tablespoons dark soy sauce

1 tablespoon Chinese rice wine or dry sherry

2 teaspoons sugar

2 tablespoons canola oil

2 teaspoons cornstarch, dissolved in 1 tablespoon water

Cilantro sprigs, for garnish

1 Cover the clams with fresh cold water and soak for about 30 minutes. Scrub the shells with a stiff brush and rinse thoroughly to remove all sand and grit. Drain. If not cooking right away, place in the refrigerator.

2 In a small bowl, combine the garlic, ginger, scallion, black beans, and chile, if using. In another small bowl, whisk together the soy sauce, wine, sugar, and ½ cup water.

3 In a wok or stir-fry pan, heat the oil over high heat. Add the black bean mixture and stir until the oil is hot and the beans sizzle. Add the clams and stir for about 30 seconds. Add the soy sauce mixture, stir to mix, and cover the pan. Cook over medium heat until the clams just open, about 5 minutes. Stir occasionally for even cooking.

4 Remove the lid and stir up the cornstarch mixture, add it to the pan, and continue stirring until thickened. Transfer the clams to a serving dish and garnish with cilantro. Serve immediately.

dry-cooked sichuan scallops

The Sichuan dry-cooked or *kan shao* method of cooking intensifies the natural flavor of scallops. You can use either bay scallops or sea scallops; if you use the smaller bay scallops, reduce the cooking time. ✳ **SERVES 3 TO 4**

---

1 pound sea scallops

1 tablespoon minced peeled fresh ginger

1 tablespoon Chinese rice wine or dry sherry

⅓ cup fermented black beans, coarsely chopped

2 garlic cloves, minced

1 tablespoon crushed red pepper, or to taste

3 tablespoons canola oil

3 tablespoons dark soy sauce

1 teaspoon sugar

1 Rinse the scallops quickly and cut in half horizontally if they are very large. Drain thoroughly and pull off the tough outer muscle. In a medium bowl, stir together the ginger and wine. Add the scallops and mix well. In a small bowl, combine the black beans, garlic, and crushed red pepper.

2 In a wok or stir-fry pan, heat the oil over medium-high heat. Add the black bean mixture to the oil and stir until the oil is hot and the beans sizzle. Don't let the garlic burn or it will become bitter.

3 Add the scallops to the pan and cook, stirring, until they turn opaque, 1 to 2 minutes. Add the soy sauce and sugar and stir for another 30 seconds to 1 minute, or until thoroughly cooked. All the liquid will have evaporated. Serve immediately.

flower squid with mixed vegetables

Squid, naturally low in fat, is an excellent choice for stir-frying, but it becomes tough and rubbery if overcooked. The squid body should be scored and blanched before stir-frying so it will cook quickly. When cooked the squid curls up like a flower bud, hence the name. ✳ **SERVES 3 TO 4**

---

1 pound fresh squid, cleaned

3 tablespoons canola oil

2 garlic cloves, crushed with the side of a knife and peeled

2 slices unpeeled fresh ginger

1 carrot, thinly sliced on the diagonal

½ green bell pepper, cored and cut into 1-inch chunks

1 cup broccoli florets

2 cups bok choy chunks

1 small onion, peeled and quartered

½ cup canned chicken broth

2 tablespoons fermented black beans, coarsely chopped

1 cup snow peas, end snapped off and strings removed

½ teaspoon salt, or to taste

2 teaspoons cornstarch dissolved in 2 tablespoons water

1 Rinse the squid thoroughly, inside and out, with cold water and drain. Cut down 1 side of the body tube and spread out flat with the inside facing up. Lightly score the flesh in a fine crisscross pattern, then cut into pieces about 2 to 3 inches square. If the head with the tentacles is large, cut it in half. Bring water to a boil in a saucepan, remove from heat, and plunge the squid in the water for 15 seconds. The squid will turn opaque and it will curl. Immediately drain in a colander and rinse in cold water to stop the cooking. Shake out excess water and drain thoroughly.

2 In a wok or stir-fry pan, heat 1 tablespoon of the oil. Add the garlic and the ginger and stir until the oil is hot and the garlic and ginger sizzle. Add all the vegetables except the snow peas and stir for about 30 seconds. Add the broth, reduce the heat to medium, cover, and cook until the vegetables are tender, 1 to 2 minutes.

3 Return the heat to high and add the blanched squid, black beans, and snow peas. Stir for 30 seconds to not more than 1 minute. Taste and add salt, as needed. Add the cornstarch mixture and stir until thickened. Remove and discard the garlic and ginger, if desired. Serve immediately.

bean curd (tofu)

bean curd family style

Nutritious, quick, and easy, the soft bean curd contrasts nicely with the mixed vegetables. For variation, use bok choy in place of green cabbage, and fresh white mushrooms for the dried black. For a spicy version, add 1 teaspoon crushed red pepper to the hoisin sauce mixture. ✳ **SERVES 3 TO 4**

---

8 pieces medium dried black mushrooms, softened in hot water for 15 minutes

1 pound firm bean curd (tofu), drained

3 tablespoons hoisin sauce

2 tablespoons dark soy sauce

3 tablespoons canola oil

2 garlic cloves, crushed with the side of a knife and peeled

2 slices unpeeled fresh ginger

½ pound green cabbage, cut into 1½-inch chunks (about 3 cups)

1 medium red or green bell pepper, cored and cut into 1½-inch chunks

1 (8 ounce) can sliced bamboo shoots, drained

1 teaspoon crushed red pepper (optional)

2 teaspoons cornstarch dissolved in ¼ cup water

1 Drain the mushrooms, and squeeze dry. Cut off the stems and discard. Slice the caps into quarters.

2 Slice the bean curd horizontally into three even pieces. Keeping the pieces together, cut through from corner to corner into four triangles. There should be a total of 12 triangular pieces.

3 In a small bowl, mix together the hoisin sauce and soy sauce with 2 tablespoons water.

4 In a wok or stir-fry pan, heat the oil over high heat. Add the garlic and ginger and stir until the oil is hot and the garlic and ginger sizzle. Add the cabbage and cook, stirring, for 3 minutes. Add the peppers, bamboo shoots, and mushrooms, and cook, stirring, for 2 minutes. It is all right if the cabbage begins to brown slightly.

5 Add the hoisin sauce mixture, bean curd, and crushed red pepper, if using, to the pan and cook, stirring gently so the bean curd doesn't break into pieces, until heated through, about 2 minutes. Add the cornstarch mixture and stir until the sauce thickens and the ingredients are thoroughly coated, about 30 seconds more. Remove and discard the ginger and garlic, if desired. Serve immediately.

stir-fried bean curd with fresh mushrooms in oyster sauce

This is one of my favorite stir-fry dishes. Use a good-quality oyster sauce since that is what gives this quick and easy dish its robust flavor. ✳ **SERVES 4**

---

6 ounces white mushrooms

2 tablespoons dark soy sauce

2 teaspoons Chinese rice wine or dry sherry

1 teaspoon sugar

2 tablespoons oyster sauce

1 teaspoon cornstarch dissolved in 1 tablespoon water

2 tablespoons canola oil

2 garlic cloves, crushed with the side of a knife and peeled

2 slices unpeeled fresh ginger

1½ pounds firm bean curd (tofu), drained and cut into ½-inch cubes

3 scallions, thinly sliced

2 teaspoons sesame oil

1 Trim the ends of the mushrooms and slice ¼ inch thick.

2 In a small bowl, mix together the soy sauce, wine, sugar, oyster sauce, and 1 tablespoon water.

3 In a wok or stir-fry pan, heat the canola oil over high heat. Add the garlic and ginger and stir until the oil is hot and the garlic and ginger sizzle. Add the mushrooms and cook, stirring, until they turn a darker color, about 2 minutes. Add the bean curd and soy sauce mixture and cook, stirring gently but constantly for about 3 minutes. Stir in the scallions and cook for about 30 seconds more. Add the cornstarch mixture and stir until thickened. Drizzle with sesame oil and mix well. Remove and discard the garlic and ginger, if desired. Serve immediately.

bean curd with crabmeat

A light dish that allows the subtle flavor of crab to come through—a pleasant change from the usual bean curd dishes with dark sauces. ✳ **SERVES 3 TO 4**

---

1 pound firm bean curd (tofu), drained

¾ cup fresh lump or 1 (6-ounce) can crabmeat, drained

1 teaspoon Chinese rice wine or dry sherry

3 tablespoons canola oil

2 slices unpeeled fresh ginger

1 cup canned chicken broth

2 tablespoons cornstarch dissolved in ¼ cup water

1 large egg white, lightly beaten

½ teaspoon salt, or to taste

3 tablespoons thinly sliced scallions

1 Cut the bean curd into 1-inch cubes. In a medium bowl, mix the crabmeat with the wine.

2 In a wok or stir-fry pan, heat the oil over medium-high heat. Add the ginger and stir until the oil is hot and the ginger sizzles. Stir up the crabmeat mixture and add to the pan. Add the broth and stir gently. Add the bean curd and simmer over medium-low heat for about 4 minutes.

3 Raise the heat to high and when the mixture comes to a boil, slowly add the cornstarch mixture and stir until thickened. When the mixture just begins to boil again, gently stir in the egg white. Remove the pan from the heat. Taste, and add salt as needed. Remove and discard the ginger, if desired. Transfer to a serving dish and sprinkle with the scallions. Serve immediately.

grandmother's spicy bean curd

This classic Sichuan dish is called *Ma Po Doufu* in Chinese. Translated literally, it means "pockmarked grandmother's bean curd," presumably named after the woman who created it. The Japanese-style tofu (soft bean curd, not silken) is preferred for this dish. It has a smooth, tender consistency. For a vegetarian dish, omit the ground meat. ✳ **SERVES 3 TO 4**

---

2 tablespoons hot bean paste

1 tablespoon dark soy sauce

2 teaspoons Chinese rice wine or dry sherry

1 garlic clove, peeled and minced

1 teaspoon grated peeled fresh ginger

½ teaspoon crushed red pepper, or to taste

1 teaspoon Sichuan peppercorns, toasted and ground (see Note for Kung Pao Chicken, page 34)

3 tablespoons canola oil

4 ounces ground pork or beef (½ cup)

1 cup canned chicken broth or water

1 pound soft bean curd (tofu), drained and cut into 1-inch cubes

2 teaspoons cornstarch dissolved in 2 teaspoons water

2 tablespoons thinly sliced scallions

1 teaspoon sesame oil

1 In a small bowl, stir together the hot bean paste, soy sauce, wine, garlic, and ginger. In another small bowl, combine the crushed red pepper and ground peppercorns.

2 In a wok or stir-fry pan, heat the canola oil over medium-high heat until hot but not smoking. Test by adding a small piece of ground meat to the oil; it should sizzle. Add the ground meat and cook, stirring, until it separates into small pieces. Add the hot bean paste mixture and stir a few times. Add the broth and pepper mixture and stir a few times to mix. Add the bean curd. Stir gently to combine and bring the mixture to a boil. Reduce the heat to low and simmer, uncovered, until the liquid is reduced by about a quarter, 5 to 6 minutes.

3 Add the cornstarch mixture and stir until the sauce is thickened. Transfer to a rimmed platter and sprinkle with the scallions and drizzle with the sesame oil. Serve immediately.

braised bean curd
with broccoli

Serve this meatless dish as an entrée alone or with white or brown rice for a well-balanced meal. Or use it as a vegetable dish in a multicourse dinner. For deep-frying the bean curd, I use a method I call shallow-frying that calls for only one cup of oil. You can substitute store-bought deep-fried bean curd in this recipe. ✳ **SERVES 3 TO 4**

---

1 pound firm bean curd (tofu), drained

1 cup canola oil

1 pound broccoli

2 tablespoons dark soy sauce

2 tablespoons fermented black beans, coarsely chopped

2 teaspoons Chinese rice wine or dry sherry

1 teaspoon sugar

2 garlic cloves, peeled and thinly sliced

1 (8-ounce) can sliced bamboo shoots, drained

1 tablespoon cornstarch dissolved in 2 tablespoons water

1 Slice the bean curd horizontally into three even pieces. Keeping the pieces together, cut through from corner to corner into four triangles. You should have a total of 12 triangles. Blot with paper towels and set aside to drain on paper towels for 15 minutes or more.

2 Trim and peel the broccoli stalks. Chop the flower heads from the stalks and cut into florets. Slice the peeled stalks into bite-size pieces. You should have about 4 cups.

3 In a small bowl, whisk together the soy sauce, black beans, wine, sugar, and ½ cup water.

4 In a wok or stir-fry pan, heat the oil over medium-high heat until it registers 350°F on a deep-fry or candy thermometer. Slip half the bean curd into the hot oil and fry until golden brown. Turn and fry the other side. When both sides are lightly browned (this should take 10 to 15 minutes), remove from the oil with chopsticks, tongs, or a wire strainer and place on a plate lined with a double layer of paper towels. Repeat with remaining bean curd.

5 Reserve 2 tablespoons of the cooking oil and discard the rest. Place 1 tablespoon of the reserved oil in the same pan used to cook the bean curd and heat the oil over high heat until it is hot. Add the broccoli and cook, stirring, for about 30 seconds. Add ¼ cup water, reduce the heat to medium, cover, and continue cooking for another minute or two, or until tender-crisp. Remove and spread on a plate.

6 Add the second tablespoon of the reserved oil to the same pan and add the garlic. Stir around the pan until fragrant and sizzling, but do not let it burn. Add the bamboo shoots, soy sauce mixture, and fried bean curd to the pan and cook, stirring, over medium-high to high heat for 1 to 2 minutes.

7 Return the broccoli to the pan and stir fry a few times. When the liquid boils, add the cornstarch mixture and stir until the sauce thickens. Serve immediately.

vegetables

vegetarian's delight

This recipe can be a flexible combination of vegetables. I don't recommend stir-frying as an excuse for cleaning out the refrigerator, but we often find ourselves with little bits and pieces of vegetables that are not enough to make anything on their own. I use chicken bouillon cubes or powder dissolved in water when I want a more savory taste. You can use homemade or canned broth instead. Adjust the salt accordingly. ✳ **SERVES 6**

---

3 tablespoons canola oil

2 slices unpeeled fresh ginger

1 garlic clove, crushed with the side of a knife and peeled

7 to 8 cups mixed vegetables, such as broccoli, cauliflower, zucchini, summer squash, green beans, bell peppers, carrots, bamboo shoots, and water chestnuts

1 chicken bouillon cube, dissolved in ⅓ cup hot water

½ teaspoon salt, or to taste

3 teaspoons cornstarch dissolved in 2 tablespoons water

1 In a wok or stir-fry pan, heat the oil over high heat. Add the ginger and garlic and stir until the oil is hot and the ginger and garlic sizzle. Stir a few times and add the vegetables, the harder root vegetables first and the more tender ones last.

2 Add the bouillon, cover the pan, and cook over medium heat, stirring occasionally, until the vegetables are tender crisp, 1 to 2 minutes.

3 Uncover the pan, season with salt to taste, mix in the cornstarch mixture, and stir until thickened. Remove and discard the ginger and garlic, if desired. Serve immediately.

stir-fried asparagus

Although asparagus is not indigenous to China, the Chinese have added it to their repertoire and use it in many dishes. This simple stir-fry relies on the sweet freshness of springtime asparagus for flavor rather than on heavy spices. It's a dish that pairs well with Western foods like grilled fish or chicken. ✳ **SERVES 4**

---

1 pound asparagus

2 tablespoons canola oil

2 garlic cloves, thinly sliced

½ teaspoon salt, or to taste

1 red bell pepper, cored and sliced into 1½-inch long strips

1¼ teaspoons cornstarch dissolved in 1 tablespoon water

1 Snap or cut off the tough ends of the asparagus and if desired, strip off the small leaves on the spear up to 2 inches from the tip. Cut on the diagonal into 1½-inch lengths.

2 In a wok or stir-fry pan, heat the oil over high heat. Add the garlic and salt and stir until the oil is hot and the garlic sizzles. Add the asparagus and stir for about 1 minute. Add ½ cup water and cook, covered, over medium-high heat until the asparagus are tender-crisp, about 2 minutes.

3 Add the red pepper and stir until the pepper loses its raw look, 30 seconds to 1 minute. Stir up the cornstarch mixture and add it to the pan, stirring until the liquid thickens. Remove from the heat, taste, and add salt as needed. Serve immediately.

broccoli in oyster sauce

The rich flavors of the oyster sauce and dark soy sauce will not overpower the broccoli. For an interesting variation, try using Chinese broccoli, called *gan lan*, available in Asian markets. ✳ **SERVES 4 TO 5**

1½ pounds broccoli

3 tablespoons oyster sauce

1 tablespoon dark soy sauce

1 teaspoon sugar

1 teaspoon cornstarch

2 tablespoons canola oil

1 garlic clove, crushed with the side of a knife and peeled

¼ cup canned chicken broth or water

1 Trim and peel the broccoli stalks. Chop the flower heads from the stalks and cut into florets. Split the stalks in half, if thick, and cut on the diagonal into bite-size pieces. You should have about 6 cups.

2 In a small bowl, mix together the oyster sauce, soy sauce, sugar, cornstarch, and 3 tablespoons water.

3 In a wok or stir-fry pan, heat the oil over high heat. Add the garlic and stir until the oil is hot and the garlic sizzles. Add the broccoli to the pan, stirring until the pieces turn a darker green. Add the broth to the pan, reduce the heat to medium, cover, and steam until the broccoli is tender-crisp, 4 to 6 minutes.

4 Stir up the oyster sauce mixture and add it to pan. Stir until the sauce is thickened and the broccoli is completely coated. Remove and discard the garlic, if desired. Transfer to a platter and serve immediately.

stir-fried napa cabbage

Here's a simple family-style vegetable dish. You could use other kinds of Chinese cabbage, but I prefer napa cabbage, not only for its delicate flavor and texture, but also because it keeps very well in the refrigerator and makes a perfect emergency ingredient. You can use homemade or canned broth instead of the bouillon cube. Adjust the salt accordingly. ✳ **SERVES 4**

---

1 pound napa cabbage

2 tablespoons canola oil

2 slices unpeeled fresh ginger

1 chicken bouillon cube dissolved in ½ cup hot water

1½ teaspoons cornstarch dissolved in 2 tablespoons water

1 Remove and discard any tough, wilted, or discolored leaves from the cabbage. Cut the cabbage lengthwise into 2-inch wide wedges. Cut out the core and cut the wedges crosswise into 3-inch lengths. Separate the leaves.

2 In a wok or stir-fry pan, heat the oil over high heat. Add the ginger and stir until the oil is hot and the ginger sizzles. Add the cabbage and cook, stirring, about 2 minutes.

3 Add the bouillon to the pan, stir a couple of times, and reduce the heat to medium. Cover and cook, stirring occasionally, until the desired tenderness is achieved, about 2 minutes. If too much of the liquid evaporates, add a few tablespoons of water. There must be liquid in the pan to bind with the cornstarch.

4 Uncover the pan, turn the heat to high, and add the cornstarch mixture. Stir until the liquid is thickened. Remove and discard the ginger, if desired. Serve immediately.

➨ **VARIATION:** Add ¼ cup dried shrimp, rinsed and drained, to the cabbage when adding the broth in step 3.

stir-fried cauliflower and broccoli

The contrasting colors of these two vegetables make a simple dish special. You could also use only one vegetable with, perhaps, a garnish of two tablespoons minced Smithfield ham for color and flavor. ✳ **SERVES 3 TO 4**

½ **pound cauliflower**

½ **pound broccoli**

2 tablespoons canola oil

1 garlic clove, crushed with the side of a knife and peeled

½ **cup canned chicken broth or water**

½ **teaspoon salt**

2 teaspoons cornstarch dissolved in 2 tablespoons water

1 Cut the cauliflower into bite-size pieces. Trim and peel the broccoli stalks. Chop the flower heads from the stalks and cut into florets. Slice the peeled stalks into bite-size pieces.

2 In a wok or stir-fry pan, heat the oil over high heat. Add the garlic and stir until the oil is hot and the garlic sizzles. Add the cauliflower and cook, stirring, for about 2 minutes. Add the broccoli and cook, stirring, for 1 minute more.

3 Add the broth and cover. Turn the heat to medium and simmer, stirring occasionally, until the vegetables are tender-crisp, 4 to 6 minutes, or longer if you like the vegetables more tender.

4 Uncover the pan, sprinkle with salt, and stir to mix thoroughly. Turn the heat to high, add the cornstarch mixture, and stir until the gravy thickens. Remove and discard the garlic, if desired. Serve immediately.

shanghai bok choy with black mushrooms

You'll probably have to make a trip to a Chinese market to find Shanghai bok choy but these tender little cabbages with their lovely jade color and delicate flavor are well worth the effort. In China, the hearts of Shanghai bok choy are considered a delicacy and are often served at banquets. ✳ **SERVES 2**

---

8 medium dried black mushrooms

1 tablespoon light soy sauce

1 teaspoon sugar

½ teaspoon Chinese rice wine or dry sherry

½ teaspoon salt

Dash freshly ground black pepper

½ pound Shanghai bok choy

2 tablespoons canola oil

1 slice unpeeled ginger

1 (8-ounce) can sliced bamboo shoots, drained (optional)

2 teaspoons cornstarch dissolved in 2 tablespoons water

1 Soak the mushrooms in hot water for 15 minutes to soften. Drain the mushrooms and squeeze dry, reserving 1 cup of strained soaking liquid. With scissors, trim off and discard the woody stems. In a small bowl, whisk together the soy sauce, sugar, wine, salt, pepper, and reserved soaking liquid.

2 Remove and discard any wilted or discolored leaves from the bok choy. Clean thoroughly under running water. Pull the larger outer leaves from the head one by one and cut them in half or thirds lengthwise. When you reach the very tiny center leaves, cut the whole core in half or quarters to match the size of the leaves.

3 Bring 6 cups of water to a boil, add the cabbage, and blanch it for 2 minutes. Drain immediately and run under cold water to stop the cooking. Gently squeeze out the excess water and set aside.

4 In a wok or stir-fry pan, heat the oil over medium-high heat. Add the ginger and stir until the oil is hot and the ginger sizzles. Add the mushrooms, bamboo shoots, if using, cabbage leaves, and the mushroom liquid and stir until boiling. Add the cornstarch mixture and stir until thickened. Taste and add salt, as needed. Remove and discard the ginger, if desired. Serve immediately.

➨ **NOTE:** For a banquet-style presentation, arrange the cabbage leaves in a sunburst pattern on a platter. Pile the mushrooms and bamboo shoots in the center and serve.

kan shao green beans

You can also use Chinese long beans in this recipe. Break them into pieces about 1½ inches long. The texture will be a little softer. ✳ **SERVES 4**

1 pound green beans, ends snapped off and strings removed

¼ cup fermented black beans, coarsely chopped

1 tablespoon minced peeled fresh ginger

2 garlic cloves, minced

1 tablespoon crushed red pepper, or to taste

3 tablespoons canola oil

2 tablespoons light soy sauce

1 teaspoon sugar

1 Snap the green beans into pieces about 1½ to 2 inches long. Rinse in cold water and drain thoroughly.

2 In a small bowl, combine the black beans, ginger, garlic, and crushed red pepper.

3 In a wok or stir-fry pan, heat the oil over medium-high heat until hot but not smoking. Add the black bean mixture; it will sizzle slightly when added. Stir until fragrant.

4 Add the green beans, soy sauce, and sugar and stir a few times. Add ½ cup water, stir to mix, cover, and cook over medium heat for 5 minutes. Stir occasionally for even cooking. Uncover the pan, turn the heat to high, and cook until the beans are tender and the liquid has evaporated, about 5 minutes. Stir frequently to ensure even cooking and to prevent burning as the liquid evaporates. Serve immediately.

wok-seared spinach

Chinese poets describe spinach with pink roots as a "red-mouthed green parrot." My mother often took us to a farm stand and asked if we could pick spinach ourselves; that way we could pull it up with the sweet pink roots still attached. We would leave about ½ inch of the root attached, then scrape it clean with our fingernails or a small knife. Although the pink makes a prettier dish, you can use regular loose spinach. The small amount of sugar in the recipe brings back the natural sweetness of just-picked vegetables. ✳ **SERVES 2 TO 3**

---

1 pound spinach, preferably with the pink roots attached

2 tablespoons canola oil

2 garlic cloves, crushed with the side of a knife and peeled

½ teaspoon salt

1 teaspoon sugar

1 Fill the sink with cold water and put the spinach in the water. Separate the large leaves with their stalks. Leave the smaller leaves attached to the root. Scrape the pink root clean with your fingernails or a paring knife. Lift the spinach from the water and place in a colander. Discard the water and repeat the washing two more times. There should be no grit in the bottom of the sink after the last washing. Drain well and leave the spinach leaves whole.

2 In a wok or stir-fry pan, heat the oil place over high heat. Add the garlic and salt and stir until the oil is hot and the garlic sizzles.

3 Add the spinach and stir until the spinach begins to wilt. Sprinkle with the sugar and continue stirring until well wilted, 1 to 2 minutes. Spread on a shallow platter and serve immediately.

garlicky green beans

In the classic preparation of this dish the green beans are first deep-fried then stir-fried. I like to "steam" the beans in the wok first and then finish them off by stir-frying. This way the dish is less oily and the beans remain plump and fresh tasting. ✳ **SERVES 4**

---

1 pound green beans, ends snapped off and strings removed

2 tablespoons dark soy sauce

2 teaspoons sugar

1 teaspoon chili-garlic sauce or crushed red pepper, or to taste

1 teaspoon Chinese rice wine or dry sherry

3 tablespoons canola oil

2 teaspoons minced garlic

2 teaspoons minced peeled fresh ginger

¼ cup thinly sliced scallion, white parts only

1 teaspoon sesame oil

1 Snap the green beans in half. Rinse in cold water and drain thoroughly.

2 In a small bowl, combine the soy sauce, sugar, chili-garlic sauce, and wine.

3 In a wok or stir-fry pan, heat 1 tablespoon of the canola oil over high heat until the oil is hot, but not smoking. Test by dipping the end of a green bean in the oil; it should sizzle. Add the green beans and cook, stirring, for 2 minutes. Add ½ cup water, stir, and cover the pan. Reduce the heat to medium and cook, stirring occasionally, until the beans are tender-crisp, 6 to 9 minutes. Transfer the green beans to a shallow platter.

4 Add the remaining 2 tablespoons of canola oil to the same pan and heat over medium-high heat. Add the garlic, ginger, and scallions, stirring constantly until fragrant, about 15 seconds.

5 Return the green beans to the pan. Stir up the soy sauce mixture and add to the pan. Stir briskly until the liquid has nearly evaporated, about 1 minute. Drizzle with the sesame oil and mix well. Serve immediately.

mushrooms, bean sprouts, and snow peas

The Chinese like to use the number three in dishes. In Chinese this dish is known as "Three Delights." Each ingredient has a distinct texture and appearance that make the dish delightful to eat and delightful to look at. ✳ **SERVES 2 TO 3**

½ cup dried black mushrooms, softened in 2 cups hot water for 15 minutes

2 tablespoons light soy sauce

1 teaspoon sugar

3 tablespoons canola oil

½ pound snow peas, ends snapped off and strings removed

½ teaspoon salt

1 (8-ounce) can sliced bamboo shoots, drained

1½ teaspoons cornstarch dissolved in 1 tablespoon water

1 Drain the mushrooms and squeeze dry, reserving ½ cup of soaking liquid. With scissors, trim off the woody stems and discard. Slice the caps into halves or quarters, if large. In a small bowl, whisk together the reserved soaking liquid with the soy sauce and sugar.

2 In a wok or stir-fry pan, heat 2 tablespoons of the oil over high heat until hot but not smoking. Test by dipping the end of a snow pea in the oil; it should sizzle. Sprinkle in the salt, then add the snow peas and cook, stirring constantly, until the peas turn a darker green, about 1 minute. Transfer to a platter and spread out to stop cooking.

3 Add the remaining 1 tablespoon of oil to the same pan. Stir in the bamboo shoots and mushrooms with the mushroom liquid mixture. Cook, stirring, for about 2 minutes. Add the cornstarch mixture and stir until thickened. Return the snow peas to the pan and mix thoroughly. Serve immediately.

spicy sweet and sour cabbage

This dish is often served as part of a Chinese-style cold platter; it is a great choice any time your menu calls for coleslaw or sweet-and-sour red cabbage. The relish may be eaten warm, but my mother always chilled it overnight to improve the flavor and texture. ✳ **SERVES 6 TO 8 AS A SIDE DISH**

---

2 pounds napa cabbage

½ tablespoon crushed red pepper, or to taste

½ cup light brown sugar

⅓ cup cider vinegar

2 tablespoons light soy sauce

1 teaspoon salt

3 tablespoons canola oil

1 Remove and discard any wilted or discolored leaves from the cabbage. Cut it into quarters lengthwise and cut out and discard the core. Cut each quarter across into 4-inch pieces. Shred lengthwise into ½-inch-wide strips. Toss to separate the leaves.

2 In a small bowl, combine the crushed red pepper, sugar, vinegar, soy sauce, and salt.

3 In a wok or stir-fry pan, heat the oil over medium-high heat until the oil is hot but not smoking. Test by dipping a piece of cabbage into the oil; it should sizzle. Add the cabbage and stir constantly until the leaves become limp and the stems loose their raw look, about 5 minutes. Remove the pan from the heat and stir in the pepper mixture.

4 Transfer the cabbage and all the liquid to a large platter and spread it out to stop cooking. Stir occasionally to distribute the flavoring evenly. When completely cooled, lightly drain some of the liquid and serve. Or refrigerate in the liquid and drain before serving.

➡ **NOTE:** The cabbage tastes best if left to stand for at least 1 hour before draining. It may be kept in the refrigerator for several days.

ginger-glazed carrots
and parsnips

The natural sweetness of these root vegetables is enhanced by the light ginger glaze. This dish is a particularly good accompaniment for roast pork or poultry. ✳ **SERVES 4 AS A SIDE DISH**

---

2 tablespoons canola oil

4 medium carrots, cut on the diagonal into 1-inch pieces

3 medium parsnips, cut on the diagonal into 1-inch pieces

4 teaspoons light brown sugar

1 teaspoon grated peeled fresh ginger

¼ teaspoon salt

Dash of freshly ground black pepper, or to taste

1 teaspoon chopped fresh parsley

1 In a wok or stir-fry pan, heat the oil over high heat until hot but not smoking. Test by dipping a carrot piece into the oil; it should sizzle. Add the carrots and parsnips and cook, stirring, for about 2 minutes. Add ¼ cup water, reduce the heat to medium, cover, and cook, stirring occasionally, until the vegetables are tender, 5 to 6 minutes; a fork should go in easily with just a little resistance.

2 Uncover the pan and add the sugar, ginger, salt, and pepper. Turn the heat to high and stir to reduce the liquid to a glaze, 1 to 2 minutes. Transfer to a shallow platter and sprinkle with the parsley. Serve immediately.

stir-fried celery

Celery is a terrific stir-fry ingredient—crisp, low in fat, high in fiber, economical, and usually on hand in the refrigerator. Carrots add a bright color contrast to the light green celery stalks. You could also use a red bell pepper. ✳ **SERVES 4 AS A SIDE DISH**

1 pound celery

2 tablespoons canola oil

1 garlic clove, thinly sliced

½ teaspoon salt

3 carrots, peeled and cut on the diagonal ¼ inch thick

½ cup canned chicken broth

1 teaspoon cornstarch dissolved in 1 tablespoon water

1 Separate the celery stalks and wash thoroughly, paying special attention to grit in the grooves on the outside of the stalks. Trim off the leaves and a little from the root end of each stalk. String the tough outer stalks. Slice each stalk on the diagonal ½-inch thick. You should have about 4 cups.

2 In a wok or stir-fry pan, heat the oil over medium-high heat. Add the garlic and salt and stir until the oil is hot and the garlic sizzles. Add the carrots and cook, stirring, for about 1 minute.

3 Add the celery and broth, lower the heat to medium, cover, and simmer, stirring occasionally, until the vegetables are tender-crisp, 3 to 5 minutes. Uncover and add the cornstarch slurry, stirring until the liquid thickens. Taste and add salt as needed. Serve immediately.

index